Great Gingerbread

Great Gingerbread

by Sara Perry
Photographs by Frankie Frankeny

CHRONICLE BOOKS
SAN FRANCISCO

To Kathlyn Meskel and Jane Zwinger, creative cooks, culinary cohorts, and faithful companions in the search for glorious gingerbread.

ACKNOWLEDGMENTS

To my husband, Pete Perry, who gamely ignored the sticky molasses and gingerbread crumbs, go all my thanks.
Thanks also to my friends Catherine Glass and Colby Whipple, who gave generously of their time and help.

Working with Chronicle Books is always a pleasure, and editor Leslie Jonath is one of the reasons. Her enthusiasm, good ideas, and warm voice make every encounter a pleasure. Judith Dunham is a splendid copy editor, and assistant editor Sarah Putman is another kind heart whose eye for detail is always superb. And, of course, my gratitude to Bill LeBlond, senior editor at Chronicle Books, with whom I'd share a gingerbread cookie any time, any place.

Text copyright © 1997 by Sara Perry.

Photographs copyright © 1997 by Frankie Frankeny.

Library of Congress Cataloging-in-Publication Data:
Perry, Sara.
        Great gingerbread/by Sara Perry; photographs by Frankie Frankeny.
            p. cm.
        Includes index.
        ISBN 0-8118-1613-3 (pbk.)
        1. Gingerbread. I. Title
    TX771.P44 1997
    641.8'653–dc21   97-6173
                                                                         CIP

Printed in Hong Kong.

Designed by Mitten Design.
Food styling by Jackie Slade, Wesley Martin, and Laurel Corkran.
The photographer wishes to thank Laura Lovett and Bill LeBlond for another opportunity to work with Chronicle Books; Sara Perry, Marianne Mitten and Williams-Sonoma for their props, and special thanks to their staff at Stonestown, who were very generous with their time during the holiday season.

Distributed in Canada by
Raincoast Books
8680 Cambie Street
Vancouver, British Columbia V6P 6M9

10 9 8 7 6 5 4 3 2 1

Chronicle Books
85 Second Street
San Francisco, California 94105

Web Site: www.chronbooks.com

Contents

Great Gingerbread

When I hear the word *gingerbread,* I think of a platter of spicy gingerbread men dressed up with raisin eyes and frosted trousers, or a fragrant, molasses-laden cake served warm from the oven with softly whipped cream. Every year around the holidays, I remember the gingerbread houses made by our next-door neighbors, the Neumans, when I was a child living in Los Angeles. The Neumans had come from Germany. Mr. Neuman had been an artist and cabinetmaker, but in California—in the 1950s—he designed passenger planes.

✪ On dark fall evenings, Mr. Neuman's studio light would shine in my window way past my bedtime as he drew the intricate plans for the gingerbread house we would all build together. My favorite was the one that looked like the witch's house in Hansel and Gretel. My brother, Mark, liked the log cabin. Mrs. Neuman loved the house that looked like Bing Crosby's mansion in Beverly Hills, complete with a pool made of aqua sheet gelatin. ✪ It was Mrs. Neuman's job to make the dough, cut out the patterns, and bake the gingerbread pieces. It was my job to measure the spices she kept in red tins at the back of her pantry. Mark helped her roll out the dough. ✪ The day after Thanksgiving we built the gingerbread house. The house was erected on a carved wooden tray Mr. Neuman had made his wife as a wedding present. We were always full from the previous night's turkey and pumpkin pie, but that didn't stop Mark or me from filling up on the special hard candies Mrs. Neuman's sister sent from Nuremberg. Our job was to put a dot of icing on the back of each candy and stick it on as a shingle. (I later learned that Nuremberg is the home of the German gingerbread man and that for more than six hundred years Bavarian bakers have been cutting out gingerbread people and houses.) ✪ I don't remember what happened to all those gingerbread houses, or when we stopped making them together, but like many sweet memories, I still savor them. In those childhood days, gingerbread was a treat eaten on special occasions, and its history stretched back no further than last year's gingerbread house. But today, gingerbread is finding its way into all kinds of recipes, from breakfast cakes to autumn puddings, and it can be enjoyed any time of day, any season of the year.

✧ Gingerbread has an ancient history. Ginger, a highly prized, peppery spice, has been revered since the time of Confucius (551–478 B.C.), who recognized its calming effect on the digestive system and its ability to stimulate circulation. Early Greek and Roman bakers made a flat bread spiced with ginger that was consumed for digestive relief after a large meal. The Romans also relished ginger as an accent and flavoring in foods, and they spread its use throughout their territories, which include present-day Germany, France, and Great Britain. With the fall of the empire in the fifth century, ginger's use all but disappeared until spice traders and explorers like Venetian Marco Polo brought it back with other spices from Asia to Europe during the latter half of the thirteenth century. ✧ By the end of the thirteenth century, ginger was considered a valuable spice, used in everything from medicines to meal preparation. Englishmen with sensitive stomachs sucked a sweet lozenge known as *gingerbrati*. This medical marvel, a mixture of honey, ginger, nutmeg, and other spices, was not only the nobleman's antacid, but was believed to ward off diseases as serious as the plague. Bread crumbs were added to the honey-ginger mixture, and gingerbread came to mean a sweet cake flavored with honey or molasses and scented with spices. ✧ Gingerbread was the cotton candy of European festivals and fairs. Cut into the shapes of animals, letters, kings and queens, gilded with sugar—sometimes even with gold—gingerbread became synonymous with extravagant decoration. Gingerbread became so popular in England during Queen Elizabeth I's reign that the royal family employed their own gingerbread baker. Baroque bakers in what is now central Europe created splendid gingerbread confections, often using intricately shaped, wooden gingerbread molds. ✧ Gingerbread was a popular food in the North American colonies. Native Americans introduced to colonists a sweet syrup from the maple tree, and maple syrup now flavors many gingerbread recipes. By the early nineteenth century, inspired by the classic fairy tale of the Brothers Grimm, gingerbread houses fit for witches were being baked—and nibbled—on both sides of the Atlantic. Today, gingerbread continues to remind us of traditional pleasures, while offering us new tantalizing taste sensations. ✧ *Great Gingerbread* features all the different kinds of gingerbreads that make up this delicious family, from morning cakes fragrant with the traditional trinity of ginger, cinnamon, and nutmeg to sweet treats flavored with more unusual blends, like Chinese five-spice powder with its fennel and peppercorn. You'll discover there's a gingerbread for every taste and level of baking skill. I hope that many of these recipes become a part of your family's tradition.

Tips for Baking Gingerbread

Gingerbread lovers will find this book filled with many delicious recipes, from waffles and scones to gingerbread houses, cookies, and cakes. Some take just minutes to prepare and require only a bowl and a spoon. Others, like the gingerbread houses, require more equipment and benefit from a team effort. Here are some basic tips that will help you no matter which recipe you choose to make.

For the best gingerbread every time:

✶ Before you begin, read each recipe thoroughly to make sure that you have all of the ingredients and the right cooking utensils. Nothing is more irritating than learning halfway through a recipe that you're out of something.

✶ Preheat your oven for at least 15 minutes to ensure uniform heat. For proper air circulation, make sure there is plenty of air space between the pan and the oven wall. Also, since temperatures vary from one oven to another, and the actual temperature is often different from the setting, it's worth investing in a portable oven thermometer.

✶ Measure all your ingredients accurately. When you measure liquids, use a clear measuring cup and place it on a level surface. After pouring in the liquid, check the measure at eye level. When you measure dry ingredients, use a measuring cup that is exactly the volume you want, scoop the full amount, and scrape off the excess with the back of a table knife.

While many cookbooks state that sifting flour is unnecessary, I still do because I think it lightens the flour for a more accurate measurement.

✶ Do not overmix dough once you add flour or dry ingredients to a creamed mixture. Mix only until they are just blended, or the dough will become tough.

✶ Cool all baked goods thoroughly before storing. Otherwise, when they are covered or sealed, they can "sweat" and become soggy. This also applies to frosting cakes and cookies.

For the best cookies every time:

✶ Bake cookies on heavy-gauge baking sheets with low sides or no sides at all. Heavy-gauge sheets ensure uniform heat distribution and browning. The low sides make the sheets easier to grasp and also allow the air to circulate for uniform baking.

Shiny baking sheets divert heat and produce a softer bottom crust on cookies, while dark sheets absorb the heat and create a crisper bottom. Line dark sheets with aluminum foil, if you prefer a softer bottom crust.

✶ Use parchment paper as an alternative to greasing baking sheets. Parchment paper also makes cleanup easier. Made of heavy, grease- and moisture-resistant paper, it comes in rolls like waxed paper and is available in many supermarkets and gourmet shops.

✶ Spoon drop cookie dough with a *flatware* teaspoon or tablespoon, not a measuring spoon. Cookies will bake and brown evenly if they are the same size and shape.

✶ Bake cookies on a *cool* baking sheet, preferably one sheet at a time. If you find that the cookies are spreading too much as they bake, try chilling the dough or adding 1 to 2 tablespoons of flour. If they are too dry, add 1 to 2 tablespoons of milk.

✶ The first time you try a recipe, check cookies several minutes before the end of the baking time stated in the recipe. For drop cookies, press your finger on the surface of the cookie. It should leave a slight indentation. Rolled and refrigerator cookies are done when they are just turning golden brown.

✶ If you like your cookies chewy with just a touch of color, reduce the baking time by 1 or 2 minutes. If you like them crisp and crunchy, increase the baking time by 1 or 2 minutes.

Know Your Ingredients

When you compare your favorite gingerbread recipes, you'll notice right away that they share many of the same ingredients that give gingerbreads their distinctive flavors. Here is a list of the most popular ingredients, where they came from, and how they are used.

For best results with any recipe, make sure your pantry is stocked with basic flours and sugars that have been properly stored. Except for salt and granulated sugar, which will keep indefinitely if stored in a cool, dark place, it is a good idea to replace other dry ingredients every 6 months. To ensure fresh dairy products, check carton dates, and buy eggs, milk, and butter that have been stored in a refrigerator case.

Spices

Spices give any gingerbread its delicious aroma and memorable taste. For the freshest flavor, it's best to buy small amounts of spices and use them within 6 months. (Jot the date with a permanent pen on the lid of the spice jar and you'll know when to replace it.)

The best place to store your spices is in a cool, dark place, not out in the open where light and heat will affect their freshness. Whenever possible, grind your own whole spices with a spice grinder or in a mortar with a pestle; the flavor and fragrance can't be beat.

✴ **Ginger** is the spice you'll find in every gingerbread recipe. It comes from the knobby rhizome of a tropical plant and has a peppery zing and spicy scent. Ginger comes fresh, ground, or crystallized, and is used all three ways in gingerbread.

Fresh ginger, known also as gingerroot, is actually a rhizome or underground stem. It can be found year-round in the produce section of most supermarkets. When you choose a piece, the "hand" and "fingers" of the gingerroot should be plump and feel heavy and firm for their size. The tan skin should not be wrinkled. If you're not going to use it within several days, store the unpeeled rhizome in the vegetable bin of your refrigerator. For longer storage, wrap it in a plastic bag. The root will keep up to 3 weeks, but avoid keeping too long or it will turn moldy. **Ground ginger** is dried gingerroot that has been finely ground. It should not be used as a substitute in recipes calling for fresh ginger. Like other spices, dried ginger is more fragrant and flavorful if it is freshly ground. While difficult to find, dried gingerroot "hands" are sometimes available in Asian and Indian food stores and can be ground with a spice grinder. **Crystallized ginger** is sliced fresh ginger that has been cooked in sugar syrup and coated with granulated sugar. While it's often enjoyed as a candy, it can spice up gingerbread with little pockets of unexpected pleasure.

✴ **Cinnamon** comes from the inner bark of a tropical evergreen tree. Early Romans believed cinnamon was an aphrodisiac and enjoyed its sweet taste in their love potions. (Unhappy lovers also used it to calm upset stomachs.) Cinnamon is available in ground form and as pieces of bark twisted and dried into cigarettelike tubes and sold as cinnamon sticks. For baking, use ground cinnamon.

✴ **Nutmeg** comes from an egg-shaped fruit kernel and adds a nutty, sweet spiciness to gingerbread. You can purchase nutmeg already ground or in kernels. Nutmeg graters make shaving whole nutmeg an easy task. **Mace,** actually the lacy covering of the nutmeg kernel, has a light, almost cinnamonlike flavor. Mace is already ground when you buy it.

✴ **Cloves** are highly aromatic—perhaps that's one reason a Chinese emperor had all those within speaking distance of him chew the nail-shaped flower buds. Cloves can be purchased whole or already ground. To crush the whole buds, grind them in a spice grinder or in a mortar with a pestle.

* **Cardamom** is from the seed pods of a plant related to ginger and adds a perfumelike aroma and flavor to gingerbreads. Some say it resembles a gentle ginger with a touch of pine or a hint of eucalyptus. In recipes that call for whole cardamom, use the flat side of a knife to lightly crush the flavorless pod and release the seeds. To crush the seeds, grind them in a spice grinder or in a mortar with a pestle. While I use ground cardamom for cookies and cakes, I always use whole, crushed cardamom pods and their seeds to flavor liquids for custards, ice creams, and sauces.

* **Allspice** comes from the peppercorn-shaped berries of a tropical New World evergreen tree first discovered in the sixteenth century by Spaniards exploring the Mexican rain forests. The rust-colored berries have the fragrance of cloves, the flavor of cinnamon, and the pungency of nutmeg. You can purchase the berries ground or whole, and they can be crushed with a spice grinder or in a mortar with a pestle.

Sweeteners

* **Molasses** is the sweet syrup most associated with gingerbread. It is the liquid that is left over when the sugar cane juice is boiled down to remove the sugar crystals. **Light molasses,** a mild molasses, comes from the first boiling of the sugar syrup, and is often used as an ingredient in pancake and waffle syrup. **Dark molasses,** a full-flavored molasses, comes from the second boiling of the sugar syrup, and is the most popular molasses used in gingerbread recipes. **Blackstrap,** the thick, dark, and somewhat bitter molasses, is from the third and final boiling. Sometimes more difficult to locate, it can be found in natural-food or health-food stores. Blackstrap gives gingerbread recipes the dark color and strong flavor that we often associate with "grandmother's recipes." Store molasses in an airtight container. When well sealed and stored in a cool, dry place, molasses will keep for up to 2 years.

* **Honey** is made by bees from flower nectar and was the first sweetener used in gingerbread. There are countless flavors associated with honey, since each flower type adds its own subtle flavor and fragrance. Orange flower honey is the most popular type used in baking. While honey can be purchased in several forms such as comb, chunk, or spun honey, use liquid honey in all recipes. Store honey in an airtight container. When well sealed and stored in a cool, dry place, honey will keep for up to 1 year. If you refrigerate honey, or it becomes crystallized, simply warm the honey by placing it briefly in a microwave or in warm water.

* **Maple syrup** is made from the sap of the sugar maple tree, which is boiled to produce a thick syrup. While there are maple-flavored syrups on the market, pure maple syrup is far superior in taste. Maple syrup is graded according to color and flavor. The highest grade is AA or Fancy, and is light in color with a soft, smooth taste. People with food sensitivities often find maple syrup easier to tolerate than other sweeteners. To keep from molding, maple syrup should be refrigerated after opening. Once open, it is best used within 1 year.

* **Brown sugar** comes in light and dark grades and is a mixture of granulated sugar and molasses. (The darker the sugar, the stronger the flavor.) Brown sugar is moist and clingy because the molasses forms a film over the sugar crystals. When that film dries, the sugar becomes hard and lumpy. To avoid this, purchase brown sugar in plastic bags that can be tightly sealed. If you purchase brown sugar in a box, transfer it to a plastic bag. Hardened brown sugar can be softened by warming in a microwave oven for a few seconds or by slipping a wedge of apple or a piece of cloth dampened with water inside the box and resealing it for 2 days. Because it contains molasses, brown sugar is best used within 2 years.

Gingerbread Classics

Fresh Apple Gingerbread

This gingerbread is quick to put together. Watch it disappear when family and friends find it on the counter.

1 cup all-purpose flour
1 teaspoon baking soda
1 teaspoon ground ginger
½ teaspoon ground cinnamon
¼ teaspoon ground nutmeg
¼ teaspoon salt
¼ cup unsalted butter,
   cut into small pieces
⅓ cup granulated sugar
⅓ cup molasses
1 large egg, lightly beaten
1 large Granny Smith apple, peeled,
   cored, and diced
Sweetened Whipped Cream (page 71)
3 to 4 ounces Cheddar cheese, grated

PREHEAT AN OVEN TO 350 DEGREES F. POSITION A RACK IN THE center of the oven. Grease an 8-inch round cake pan, and set aside.

In a bowl, sift or stir together the flour, baking soda, ginger, cinnamon, nutmeg, and salt. In a large bowl, beat the butter, using an electric mixer, until creamy. Gradually add the sugar, beating until the mixture is light and fluffy. Stir in the molasses and egg until smooth. Stir half the dry ingredients into the butter mixture until blended. Fold in the apples, and then stir in the remaining dry ingredients.

Pour the batter into the prepared pan and smooth out with a knife. Bake until a toothpick inserted in the middle comes out clean, 25 to 30 minutes. Allow the cake to cool in the pan. Cut into wedges and top each with a dollop of whipped cream and a sprinkle of grated cheese.

SERVES 6 TO 8.

Tigertail Val's Sweet Gingerbread

In the neighborhood where I grew up in Brentwood, California, a man known as Tigertail Val wrote mysteries in his book-filled den. Val loved to bake, and my friends and I felt quite grown-up when he treated us to his gingerbread and molasses ice cream. He used two ingredients we were never allowed to touch at home: coffee and cognac. The gingerbread is sweet and mild and a favorite with my family. The ice cream is memorable with or without the cognac.

½ cup water
2 tablespoons coarsely ground
  coffee beans
1 piece fresh ginger, 1 inch long and
  1 inch in diameter, peeled and
  coarsely chopped (optional)
½ cup (1 stick) unsalted butter,
  at room temperature
1 cup firmly packed dark brown sugar
½ cup dark or blackstrap molasses
1 large egg, lightly beaten
1¼ cups all-purpose flour
½ teaspoon salt
¾ teaspoon baking soda
½ teaspoon ground ginger
½ teaspoon ground cinnamon
½ teaspoon ground nutmeg
Val's Molasses Ice Cream (page 78)

PREHEAT AN OVEN TO 350 DEGREES F. POSITION A RACK IN the center of the oven. Grease an 8-inch-square baking pan, and set aside.

In a small saucepan, combine the water, ground coffee, and fresh ginger. Bring to a rolling boil over medium heat. Remove the mixture from the heat, cover, and let steep for 5 minutes.

In a bowl, beat together the butter, brown sugar, and molasses, using an electric mixer, until smooth. Add the coffee mixture by pouring it through a fine-mesh sieve. Stir the ingredients together with a whisk. Whisk in the egg. Sift the flour, salt, baking soda, ginger, cinnamon, and nutmeg into the molasses mixture, and beat until smooth.

Pour the batter into the prepared pan and bake until a toothpick inserted in the middle comes out clean, about 30 minutes. Cool in the pan on a wire rack for 5 minutes before cutting into slices. Serve each slice with ½ cup of Val's Molasses Ice Cream.

SERVES 6 TO 8.

Mrs. Keller's Gingerbread

On the inside cover of Julia Blunt's well-worn cookbook is written the date April 22, 1905. In her same curvy penmanship on a page of the book is a recipe for Mrs. Keller's Gingerbread. The book and the recipe are now the prized possession of Julia's granddaughter, Mary Ellen Buck. Rich, dark, and moist, this heirloom gingerbread gets its old-fashioned flavor from blackstrap molasses, the thickest and most concentrated grade of molasses.

½ cup (1 stick) unsalted butter,
  at room temperature
1 cup granulated sugar
1 cup blackstrap molasses
2 large eggs, well beaten
2½ cups all-purpose flour
1 tablespoon ground ginger
1 teaspoon ground cinnamon
1 teaspoon ground cloves
1 cup boiling water
2 teaspoons baking soda
Sweetened Whipped Cream (page 71)

PREHEAT AN OVEN TO 350 DEGREES F. POSITION A RACK IN the center of the oven. Grease a 13-by-9-by-2-inch baking pan, and set aside.

In a large bowl, beat the butter and sugar, using an electric mixer, until light and creamy. Stir in the molasses until smooth. Stir in the eggs until well combined.

Sift the flour, ginger, cinnamon, and cloves into the molasses mixture, and beat until smooth.

In a small bowl, combine the boiling water and baking soda. The mixture will be foamy. Add the water to the batter, stirring until well combined. Pour the batter into the prepared pan. Bake until a toothpick inserted in the middle comes out clean, about 50 minutes. Cool in the pan on a wire rack for 5 minutes before cutting into squares. Serve warm with Sweetened Whipped Cream.

SERVES 12.

Baxtergate Gingerbread

R*ich and satisfying like a bread pudding, this moist English gingerbread has a sticky caramel topping that makes it a favorite of gingerbread fans. Nut lovers may want to sprinkle toasted pecans over the gingerbread before serving.*

1/4 cup unsalted butter,
    at room temperature
2 tablespoons dark molasses
1/4 cup granulated sugar
3/4 cup firmly packed dark brown sugar
2 large eggs, lightly beaten
1 cup all-purpose flour
1 teaspoon baking powder
1/4 teaspoon salt
1 tablespoon ground ginger
1 teaspoon ground cinnamon
1 teaspoon ground nutmeg
1 cup boiling water
1 teaspoon baking soda
3/4 cup pitted and chopped dates tossed in
    1 tablespoon flour

Sticky Topping
3 tablespoons unsalted butter
1/3 cup firmly packed dark brown sugar
2 tablespoons whipping cream

Sweetened Whipped Cream (page 71)

PREHEAT AN OVEN TO 375 DEGREES F. POSITION A RACK IN the center of the oven. Grease an 8-inch-square baking pan, and set aside.

In a large bowl, beat the butter, molasses, and granulated and brown sugars, using an electric mixer, until smooth. Beat in the eggs, one at a time. Sift the flour, baking powder, salt, ginger, cinnamon, and nutmeg into the molasses mixture, and beat until smooth. In a small bowl, combine the boiling water and baking soda. The mixture will be foamy. Add the water to the batter, stirring until well combined. Fold in the dates.

Pour the batter into the prepared pan. Slowly run a fork through the batter to make sure the dates are evenly distributed. Bake until the cake is well browned on top, about 40 minutes. Let the cake rest in the pan on a wire rack.

Place a rack 4 to 5 inches from the heat source of a broiler. Preheat the broiler.

To make the sticky topping, combine the butter, brown sugar, and whipping cream in a small saucepan over medium heat, stirring until the butter has melted. Continue to cook, stirring constantly, until the mixture thickens, about 5 minutes. Remove from the heat and pour over the warm gingerbread, letting the topping seep down the sides.

Place the gingerbread in the broiler and broil until the topping is bubbling, 30 to 40 seconds. Watch carefully so that the topping does not burn. Cut into pieces and serve warm with Sweetened Whipped Cream.

SERVES 8.

Jack Sprat Gingerbread

In the old nursery rhyme, Jack Sprat ate no fat, and reliable sources say that this recipe was one of his favorites. It has not a bit of fat. What's interesting is that his wife (you know, the one who ate no lean) loved it too, especially with bittersweet orange Bachelor's Jam (page 76).

1½ cups honey
⅓ cup defrosted orange juice concentrate
1 teaspoon vanilla extract
4 large egg whites
½ cup applesauce
¼ cup baby food prune purée
½ cup golden raisins
½ cup chopped dates
1¾ cups all-purpose flour
¾ cup whole wheat flour
1½ teaspoons baking soda
1½ teaspoons cream of tartar
½ teaspoon salt
2 teaspoons ground ginger
1½ teaspoons ground cinnamon
½ teaspoon ground nutmeg

PREHEAT AN OVEN TO 325 DEGREES F. POSITION A RACK IN THE center of the oven. Coat a 9-inch round cake pan with nonstick cooking spray or use a nonstick pan. Set aside.

In a large bowl, combine the honey, juice concentrate, vanilla, 2 egg whites, applesauce, prune purée, raisins, and dates until just blended. Sift the all-purpose and whole wheat flours, baking soda, cream of tartar, salt, ginger, cinnamon, and nutmeg into the honey-applesauce mixture, and beat until blended.

In a small bowl, lightly beat the remaining 2 egg whites and stir them into the batter until just blended.

Spread the batter in the prepared pan. Bake until a toothpick inserted in the middle comes out clean, 40 to 45 minutes. Cool in the pan on a wire rack for 10 minutes. Cut into slices and serve warm.

SERVES 6 TO 8.

Panforte

This classic holiday cake has been an Italian specialty since the Middle Ages. It is an elaboration of the early gingerbread cakes made with honey and spices like ginger, pepper, and saffron. Eaten at the end of a meal, these cakes were believed to aid digestion. Cocoa was added in the sixteenth century, when chocolate first arrived in Italy. In this version, fresh ginger flavors the sweet honey syrup, and crystallized ginger is added to the traditional selection of candied fruit peel.

¼ cup finely chopped crystallized ginger
¼ cup finely chopped crystallized orange peel
¼ cup finely chopped crystallized lemon peel
1 cup finely chopped toasted hazelnuts (see Note)
½ cup plus 1 tablespoon all-purpose flour
¼ cup unsweetened Dutch-process cocoa
½ teaspoon ground ginger
½ teaspoon ground cinnamon
½ teaspoon ground cloves
¼ teaspoon ground nutmeg
¼ teaspoon white pepper
½ cup granulated sugar
½ cup honey
1 piece fresh ginger, 1 inch long and 1 inch in diameter, peeled and coarsely chopped
Powdered sugar for dusting

PREHEAT AN OVEN TO 325 DEGREES F. POSITION A RACK IN THE center of the oven. Grease an 8-inch round cake pan. Line the bottom of the pan with parchment paper, butter the paper, and set aside.

In a large bowl, combine the crystallized ginger, orange and lemon peels, and hazelnuts. Sift into the bowl the flour, cocoa, ginger, cinnamon, cloves, nutmeg, and white pepper. Toss all the ingredients together until well combined.

In a small saucepan, combine the sugar, honey, and fresh ginger. Bring the mixture to a boil over medium heat, stirring constantly with a wooden spoon. Continue to cook, stirring constantly, for 5 minutes, or until a drop of the mixture forms a ball when dropped in a cup of ice water, about 242 degrees F on a candy thermometer. Immediately remove from the heat and stir into the nut mixture. The batter will be thick and sticky. Place in the prepared pan and smooth out with a knife. This is easy to do with well-buttered, clean hands; be careful, as the mixture will be quite warm.

Bake until the cake is firm and a toothpick inserted in the middle comes out clean, about 25 minutes. At 25 minutes, the cake will be moist and chewy; at 30 minutes, it will become dry and brittle. Turn the cake onto a wire rack and remove the parchment paper. Invert onto another wire rack that is covered with a clean piece of parchment paper. This will make it easier to cut the cake into wedges. Dust generously with powdered sugar. Let cool slightly before cutting into small wedges.

Note: To toast hazelnuts, place the shelled nuts in a shallow pan and roast in an oven preheated to 275 degrees F until the skins crack, 20 to 30 minutes. Place the nuts in a clean kitchen towel. Fold the towel over the nuts and allow the nuts to "steam" for 5 minutes. Rub the towel firmly between your hands to remove most of the skins.

SERVES 16 TO 20.

Morning Delights

Gingerbread Pancakes with Golden Pear Compote and Maple Cream

These hearty pancakes are great anytime of year, but especially when the weather turns crisp and cold. The Golden Pear Compote makes a delicious cover for the spicy cakes, which will absorb the compote syrup. The Maple Cream, with its hint of pure maple syrup, is the ideal autumn topping. If you prefer crepelike pancakes, just thin the batter with a little extra milk.

¹/₃ cup light molasses
¹/₄ cup vegetable oil
2 large eggs
2 cups milk
2¹/₄ cups all-purpose flour
¹/₂ cup whole wheat flour
2 tablespoons granulated sugar
3 teaspoons baking powder
¹/₂ teaspoon baking soda
¹/₂ teaspoon salt
1 teaspoon ground ginger
1 teaspoon ground cinnamon

Golden Pear Compote (page 73)
Maple Cream (page 73)

PREHEAT AN OVEN TO 250 DEGREES F. POSITION A RACK IN the center of the oven. Place an ovenproof dish on the rack.

In a large bowl, beat the molasses and oil, by hand or with an electric mixer, until well blended. Beat in the eggs, one at a time, then add the milk. It is important to stir all the way to the bottom of the bowl to make sure all of the ingredients are brought together. Sift the all-purpose and whole wheat flours, sugar, baking powder, baking soda, salt, ginger, and cinnamon into the egg mixture, and beat until just blended. The batter will be slightly thick and have a rich, dark caramel color.

Heat a griddle or nonstick skillet on medium-high heat until a few drops of water skip along the hot surface. Working in batches, measure out a scant ¹/₄ cup batter for each pancake. When cooking more than one pancake at a time, pour the batter so that the pancakes do not touch. Cook the first side until the edges begin to dry and bubbles begin to appear on the top surface. Turn and cook 1 minute on the second side. Place in the oven on the preheated dish to keep warm. Repeat with the remaining batter. Serve the pancakes hot with Golden Pear Compote and Maple Cream.

MAKES TWENTY 4-INCH PANCAKES.

Very nice — Emily liked them. But the batter is thick so spread it out. Burns easily because of the sugar

Cardamom Spice French Toast

*S*ummer fruits or berries make a sweet complement to this cardamom-scented French toast. Delicately sweetened with honey instead of molasses, it is reminiscent of early English gingerbread recipes. If you're a cardamom lover like I am, you may want to lavish this toast with fresh raspberries and warm Cardamom Custard Sauce (page 77). Other delicious combinations are blueberries and warm Lemon Curd (page 74) or Thompson seedless grapes tossed with Honey Cream (page 72). The Sunny Morning Relish (page 76) is a favorite of my daughter, Julie, who loves fresh fruit.

Spiced Sugar
½ cup powdered sugar
½ teaspoon ground cardamom
Pinch of ground ginger

French Toast
½ cup half-and-half
1 tablespoon honey
3 cardamom pods, split
3 large eggs
8 slices day-old French bread,
 each 1 inch thick
4 tablespoons unsalted butter

To make the spiced sugar, sift the powdered sugar, cardamom, and ginger into a small bowl, and set aside.

To make the toast, in a small saucepan, heat the half-and-half, honey, and cardamom pods over low heat. Stir occasionally until the honey is blended and the mixture is hot. Remove from the heat and let steep for 10 minutes. Strain through a fine-mesh sieve to remove the cardamom pods and seeds.

Preheat an oven to 250 degrees F. Position a rack in the center of the oven. Place an ovenproof dish on the rack.

In a small bowl, beat the eggs until combined. Whisk in the lukewarm milk and let the mixture rest for 15 minutes. Stir again to combine and pour into a shallow dish. Starting with 2 slices of bread, dip both sides of each slice into the egg mixture, making sure each slice is completely moistened but not saturated.

Melt 1 tablespoon butter in a heavy, 10-inch skillet over medium-high heat. Add the 2 slices of prepared bread. Sprinkle the top of each slice with 1 teaspoon of the spiced sugar. Cook the first side until brown. Turn and cook the second side until brown. Place in the oven on the preheated dish to keep warm. Repeat with the remaining slices and the remaining butter.

Serve the French toast hot, and sprinkle the top of each slice with 1 teaspoon of spiced sugar.

Serves 4.

Pictured on page 6.

Kathlyn's Gingerbread Waffles

This recipe was created by Kathlyn Meskel, a woman who can do anything with eggs, flour, and her imagination. Light and airy, with just the right hint of gingerbread spices, these waffles are a delightful breakfast-in-bed surprise. In the summer, all they need is a cascade of fresh blueberries and Sweetened Whipped Cream. In the winter, try the hot Spiced Blueberry Sauce (page 77) or the Sunny Morning Relish (page 76).

3 large eggs, separated
$\frac{1}{3}$ cup light or dark molasses
1 cup milk
$\frac{1}{2}$ cup unsalted butter, melted
$\frac{1}{2}$ teaspoon vanilla extract
2 cups all-purpose flour
1 tablespoon baking powder
$\frac{1}{2}$ teaspoon salt
1 tablespoon ground ginger
1 tablespoon ground cinnamon
1 teaspoon ground nutmeg
2 cups (1 pint) fresh blueberries
Sweetened Whipped Cream (page 71)

PREHEAT A WAFFLE IRON AND, IF NECESSARY, GREASE LIGHTLY. Preheat an oven to 250 degrees F. Position a rack in the center of the oven. Place an ovenproof dish on the rack.

In a large bowl, beat the egg yolks until slightly thick. In a saucepan, combine the molasses, milk, and butter over low heat and cook, stirring occasionally, until the butter melts and the mixture is blended. Remove from the heat and allow the mixture to cool to lukewarm. Stir in the vanilla. (The lukewarm mixture may appear to curdle slightly.) In a steady stream, pour the molasses mixture into the egg yolks while using a whisk to combine the ingredients. Sift the flour, baking powder, salt, ginger, cinnamon, and nutmeg into the molasses mixture, and stir until almost blended.

In a bowl, using an electric mixer, beat the egg whites until stiff but not dry. Gently fold them into the batter until just blended.

Working in batches, spoon the batter into the waffle iron. Bake until the steaming stops, about 5 minutes. Remove the waffles carefully and place in the oven on the preheated dish to keep warm. Repeat with the remaining batter.

Serve the waffles hot with blueberries and whipped cream.

MAKES EIGHT $4\frac{1}{2}$-INCH WAFFLES.

Gingerbread Jammies

T hese breakfast muffins have always been a favorite of my children. When Matthew and Julie were little, they were always surprised to find the warm raspberry jam hiding in the center. Let the muffins cool slightly before serving so that small mouths don't get burned by the hot jam.

1 cup applesauce
¼ cup vegetable oil
¼ cup firmly packed dark brown sugar
1 large egg, lightly beaten
2 cups all-purpose flour
2 teaspoons baking powder
½ teaspoon salt
1 teaspoon ground ginger
1½ teaspoons ground cinnamon
⅛ teaspoon ground cloves
⅓ cup raspberry jam

Cinnamon Sugar
½ teaspoon cinnamon
2 tablespoons granulated sugar

PREHEAT AN OVEN TO 350 DEGREES F. POSITION A RACK IN THE center of the oven. Grease 12 standard muffin cups or line with paper liners, and set aside.

To make the muffins, in a large bowl, combine the applesauce, oil, brown sugar, and egg until blended. Sift the flour, baking powder, salt, ginger, cinnamon, and cloves into the applesauce mixture, and beat until just combined.

Spoon the batter into the prepared muffin cups, filling each halfway. Spoon 1 teaspoon of jam on top of each portion of batter, and top with the remaining batter, dividing it among the muffin cups.

To make the cinnamon sugar, combine the cinnamon and sugar in a small bowl.

Sprinkle ½ teaspoon of the cinnamon sugar over each muffin top. Bake until golden brown, about 35 minutes. Let cool in the pan for 5 minutes. Serve warm.

MAKES 12 MUFFINS.

Blueberry Honey-Crunch Muffins

With their crunchy cinnamon topping, these gingerbread muffins are always the first to go at any breakfast gathering. The recipe is adapted from a delicious muffin created by Joyce and Gary Wells, who own a blueberry farm near the Columbia Gorge in Oregon. They suggest having enough blueberries on hand to make a second batch.

1 cup milk
¼ cup dark molasses
2 ½ cups all-purpose flour
1 teaspoon ground cinnamon
½ teaspoon ground ginger
¼ teaspoon ground mace
4 teaspoons baking powder
¼ teaspoon salt
¼ cup unsalted butter, softened
⅓ cup granulated sugar
1 large egg
1 teaspoon vanilla extract
2 cups fresh blueberries, dusted with
  flour (see Note)

Topping
½ teaspoon ground cinnamon
½ cup granulated sugar
⅓ cup all-purpose flour
¼ cup unsalted butter, cut into
  small pieces

TO MAKE THE MUFFINS, IN A SMALL SAUCEPAN, HEAT THE MILK and molasses over low heat, stirring until the molasses completely blends into the milk. Remove from the heat, cool to lukewarm, and set aside.

Preheat an oven to 375 degrees F. Position a rack in the center of the oven. Grease 12 standard muffin cups or line with paper liners, and set aside.

In a bowl, sift or stir together the flour, cinnamon, ginger, mace, baking powder, and salt. In a large bowl, beat the butter and sugar using an electric mixer, until light and creamy. Beat in the egg and vanilla until well blended. Stir in the dry ingredients alternately with the milk, beginning and ending with the dry ingredients. The batter will be thick. Gently fold in the blueberries. Spoon the batter into the prepared muffin cups, filling each two-thirds full.

To make the topping, in a small bowl, combine the cinnamon, sugar, flour, and butter until the mixture is crumbly.

Sprinkle the topping evenly over the muffins. Bake until golden brown, 20 to 25 minutes. Let cool in the pan for 5 minutes. Serve warm.

Note: Dusting blueberries with flour after rinsing and draining them well helps prevent the berries from "bleeding" into the muffins.

MAKES 12 MUFFINS.

Lemon Gingerbread Gems

*T*hese miniature muffins have a lovely scent of ginger and spice. Bite-sized, they're just right to serve as a treat for friends with a steaming cup of morning coffee or at formal teas. While lemon curd is traditionally used as a pastry filling, it's just right for these small muffins. If you're in a hurry or lemon curd is unavailable, it's easy to achieve a sweet lemony flavor by finishing the muffins with the lemon glaze below.

1/2 cup vegetable shortening, cut into small pieces
1/2 cup granulated sugar
1 large egg
1/2 cup milk
1 1/2 cups all-purpose flour
1 teaspoon ground ginger
1 teaspoon ground cinnamon
1 teaspoon ground cloves
1 1/2 teaspoons baking powder
1/2 teaspoon salt
1/2 cup finely chopped hazelnuts
3/4 cup purchased lemon curd or homemade Lemon Curd (page 74)

PREHEAT AN OVEN TO 350 DEGREES F. POSITION A RACK IN THE center of the oven. Grease 24 small (about 1 3/4-inch diameter) muffin cups or line with paper liners, and set aside.

In a large bowl, beat together the shortening and sugar, using an electric mixer, until light and creamy. Blend in the egg and milk. Sift the flour, ginger, cinnamon, cloves, baking powder, and salt into the shortening mixture, and beat until just combined. Stir in the nuts.

Spoon the batter into the prepared muffin cups, filling each halfway. Spoon 1/2 teaspoon of lemon curd on top of each portion of batter, and top with the remaining batter, dividing it evenly among the muffin cups. Bake until golden, about 20 minutes. Let cool in the pan for 5 minutes. Serve warm.

Variation: To make a lemon glaze, in a small bowl, blend together 3/4 cup sifted powdered sugar, 1 tablespoon freshly squeezed lemon juice, and 1 tablespoon melted butter. Drizzle over the top of each baked muffin.

MAKES 24 MUFFINS.

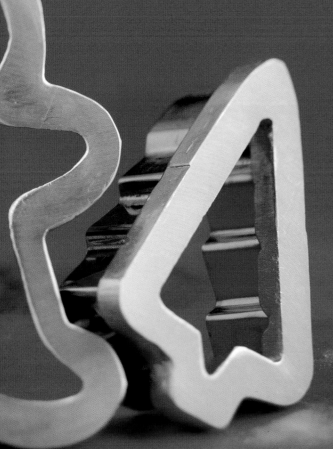

Cookies and Snaps

Gingerbread Sugar Crinkles

C ookie lovers and cookie bakers may remember making these crackle-topped treats when they were young. This recipe adds white pepper for a little extra zip.

¹/₂ cup vegetable shortening, cut into
    small pieces
¹/₄ cup unsalted butter, cut into small pieces
³/₄ cup firmly packed brown sugar
¹/₄ cup dark or blackstrap molasses
1 large egg
2¹/₄ cups all-purpose flour
2 teaspoons baking soda
¹/₂ teaspoon salt
1¹/₂ teaspoons ground ginger
1 teaspoon ground cinnamon
¹/₂ teaspoon ground cloves
¹/₂ teaspoon white pepper
¹/₄ cup granulated sugar

IN A LARGE BOWL, BEAT TOGETHER THE SHORTENING, BUTTER, AND brown sugar, using an electric mixer, until light and creamy. Beat in the molasses and egg. Sift the flour, baking soda, salt, 1 teaspoon ginger, cinnamon, cloves, and white pepper into the molasses mixture, and beat until well blended. Cover the bowl with plastic wrap and chill for 2 hours. (When tightly sealed, the dough will keep for up to 1 week in the refrigerator. If the dough becomes too cold or stiff to work easily, let it sit at room temperature until pliable, about 30 minutes.)

Preheat an oven to 375 degrees F. Position a rack in the center of the oven. Grease 2 baking sheets or line with parchment paper, and set aside.

Combine the remaining ¹/₂ teaspoon ginger with the granulated sugar in a small bowl. With clean hands, form the chilled batter into 1-inch balls (the size of large malted milk balls). Dip the top of each ball in the ginger-sugar mixture and place, sugar side up, on the prepared sheets about 2¹/₂ inches apart. Flatten each cookie with the bottom of a glass. Sprinkle the cookies with drops of water or mist them with a fine sprayer.

Bake until the tops are firm when lightly touched, 6 to 8 minutes. Let the cookies cool slightly on the baking sheets before transferring to a wire rack to cool completely. Store in an airtight container.

MAKES ABOUT 5 DOZEN COOKIES.

Chocolate Chip Gingerbread Cookies

*E*verybody's favorite cookie has got to be chocolate chip. In fact, entire books are dedicated to perfecting the national treasure created by Ruth Wakefield in the 1930s when she added some chopped chocolate to her favorite butter cookie. Here's a recipe for gingerbread lovers who crave those semisweet morsels, paired with the taste of molasses, ginger, and cinnamon.

1 cup unsalted butter,
  at room temperature
1 cup firmly packed light or
  dark brown sugar
¼ cup plus 2 tablespoons light or
  dark molasses
2 large eggs
Zest of 1 small orange, finely chopped
2½ cups all-purpose flour
1 teaspoon baking soda
½ teaspoon salt
1 teaspoon ground ginger
2 teaspoons ground cinnamon
⅔ cup semisweet chocolate chips
⅔ cup chopped walnuts

PREHEAT AN OVEN TO 375 DEGREES F. POSITION A RACK IN the center of the oven. Grease or line with parchment paper 2 baking sheets, and set aside.

In a large bowl, beat together the butter and brown sugar, using an electric mixer, until light and creamy. Beat in the molasses, eggs, and orange zest. Sift the flour, baking soda, salt, ginger, and cinnamon into the molasses mixture, and beat until blended. Stir in the chocolate chips and walnuts until well combined.

Drop the batter by rounded teaspoonfuls about 1½ inches apart on a prepared baking sheet. Bake until the cookies have set, about 12 minutes. Let the cookies cool slightly on the baking sheets before transferring them to a wire rack to cool completely. Store in an airtight container.

MAKES ABOUT 4 DOZEN COOKIES.

Lacy Flower Cookies

These delicate cookies are usually cooled into round, lacy disks. In this recipe, each cookie is pinched together at the center to resemble an open poppy. For years, whenever I made these cookies, my children informed me that it was their job to pinch the cookies. Perhaps that's one reason they are a favorite with both the after-school gang and the grown-up crowd.

⅓ cup all-purpose flour
2 teaspoons ground ginger
2 teaspoons ground cinnamon
½ teaspoon ground cloves
Pinch of salt
½ cup unsalted butter
¼ cup firmly packed brown sugar
2 tablespoons molasses

PREHEAT AN OVEN TO 350 DEGREES F. POSITION A RACK IN THE center of the oven. Line 2 baking sheets with aluminum foil, grease the foil, and set aside.

In a small bowl, sift or stir together the flour, ginger, cinnamon, cloves, and salt. In a heavy saucepan, combine the butter, sugar, and molasses over medium heat. Stir with a wooden spoon until the sugar dissolves. Do not let the mixture boil. Continue to cook at a simmer *without* stirring for 2 minutes. Remove from the heat and stir in the dry ingredients.

Drop the mixture by teaspoonfuls 2½ inches to 3 inches apart on the prepared sheets. Bake only 4 cookies at a time. Bake until lightly browned, about 7 minutes. Remove from the oven and let the cookies cool a little over 1 minute, until they can be easily handled but are still warm to the touch.

To form each cookie, lift from the baking sheet with a metal spatula. Gently pinch the center with your fingers. Cool for 1 minute, propped against the handle of a wooden spoon. Transfer to a wire rack to cool completely. If the cookies harden on the baking sheet before shaping, reheat them in the oven about 1 minute or until softened.

To retain their crispness, these cookies are best made on the day they are served. If necessary, they can be stored in an airtight container for up to 3 days.

MAKES ABOUT 2 DOZEN COOKIES.

Gingerbread Men

This recipe for gingerbread cookies is my favorite, and it's one you can adapt to your own taste. By using light or dark molasses and brown sugar, you can alter the color of the cookies. You can also adjust the spiciness by altering the amount of ginger, cinnamon, cloves, and nutmeg. ✿ While these cookies are made to be eaten, they're also perfect for hanging on a Christmas tree or using as name tags on presents or as place cards at a birthday party or holiday get-together. ✿ You can also make simple puzzles. First, cut a large square of rolled-out dough—or use a heart-shaped cookie cutter—and, with a sharp paring knife, divide it into several pieces before baking. Never has a broken heart been so delicious.

½ cup vegetable shortening
¾ cup firmly packed light or dark
*   brown sugar*
½ cup light or dark molasses
1 large egg
2 ¼ cups all-purpose flour
¼ teaspoon baking soda
½ teaspoon salt
2 teaspoons ground ginger
1 teaspoon ground cinnamon
½ teaspoon ground cloves
¼ teaspoon ground nutmeg
Drinking straw or large skewer
*   for making holes (optional)*
Raisins and nonmelting candies
*   for decorating*
Decorative Icing (page 70)

IN A LARGE BOWL, BEAT THE SHORTENING AND SUGAR WITH an electric mixer until light and fluffy. Beat in the molasses and egg until well blended. Gradually sift the flour, baking soda, salt, ginger, cinnamon, cloves, and nutmeg into the molasses mixture, and beat until blended. The dough will be sticky. Divide the dough into 4 balls, cover each ball with waxed paper or plastic wrap, and chill for at least 3 hours. (When tightly sealed, the dough will keep for up to 1 week in the refrigerator. If the dough is wrapped in freezer-weight plastic bags or aluminum foil, it can be frozen for up to 6 months. To thaw, transfer the wrapped dough to the refrigerator for 2 hours before baking or let the wrapped dough stand at room temperature for 30 minutes.)

Preheat an oven to 350 degrees F. Position a rack in the center of the oven. Line 2 baking sheets with parchment paper or leave ungreased, and set aside.

On a lightly floured board, roll one of the chilled balls of dough ¼ inch thick. Lightly dip a cookie cutter in flour (this makes it easier to release the cookie) and press it straight down into the dough. Press the edges of the cutter to make sure it has cut through the dough evenly. Cut cookies close together to avoid rerolling. The excess dough can be saved and rerolled once, but the cookies will be tougher.

With a spatula, gently transfer each cookie to the baking sheets. If a cookie is to be hung, use a drinking straw or large skewer to press a hole through the top. If not frosting the cookies, you may decorate them with raisins or nonmelting candies before baking by gently pressing them into the dough.

Bake until the cookies are set, 8 to 10 minutes. Let the cookies rest on the sheets for 2 minutes before transferring to a wire rack to cool completely.

Decorate the cooled cookies with Decorative Icing using a decorating bag (see page 91 for tips on using a decorating bag). To add raisins and decorative candies after baking, dot the candies with icing and gently press them onto the cookie. Let the cookies dry on a wire rack until the icing is set, 20 to 30 minutes. Store in an airtight container, separating successive layers with sheets of waxed paper.

MAKES ABOUT 6 DOZEN COOKIES.

Oatmeal Raisin Cookies

These chewy drop cookies are my sentimental favorites. They're the first cookies I remember baking with my mother. She had me add the measured shortening, brown sugar, raisins, and water to the bottom of a double boiler. After scooting me up to the stove on our sturdy kitchen stool, she turned on a burner to the warm setting and let me stir the concoction with an old wooden spoon until everything was melted and the raisins were plump. It seemed to take forever, but I didn't care, because I knew that afterward she'd let me help her spoon the dough onto the cookie sheets. Now, every time I make these cookies, I follow the same procedure, right down to using one pot and that old wooden spoon.

³/₄ cup raisins
¹/₂ cup vegetable shortening
¹/₄ cup water
¹/₄ cup molasses
³/₄ cup firmly packed brown sugar
³/₄ cup all-purpose flour
1 teaspoon ground ginger
¹/₂ teaspoon ground cinnamon
¹/₄ teaspoon ground nutmeg
¹/₂ teaspoon salt
¹/₂ teaspoon baking soda
1¹/₂ cups rolled oats

PREHEAT AN OVEN TO 350 DEGREES F. POSITION A RACK IN the center of the oven. Grease 2 baking sheets or line with parchment paper.

In a large saucepan over low heat, combine the raisins, shortening, water, molasses, and brown sugar. Allow the shortening to melt, stirring occasionally, until the ingredients are combined and the raisins have plumped. Remove from the heat, and immediately sift in the flour, ginger, cinnamon, nutmeg, salt, and baking soda. Stir until well blended. Stir in the rolled oats.

Drop the batter by level tablespoonfuls about 2¹/₂ inches apart on the prepared sheets. Bake until the cookies have set, about 12 minutes. Let the cookies cool slightly on the baking sheets before transferring to a wire rack to cool completely. Store in an airtight container.

MAKES ABOUT 2¹/₂ DOZEN COOKIES.

Cardamom Ginger Crisps

These crisp, spicy cookies disappear quickly whenever I make them, and I make them often because I can mix the dough quickly, wrap it, and store it in the refrigerator to slice and bake another day. Sometimes I toast the almonds to give the cookies an even richer flavor.

1 ½ cups all-purpose flour
1 teaspoon baking soda
3 teaspoons plus 1 teaspoon
   ground cardamom
½ teaspoon ground ginger
¼ teaspoon ground nutmeg
¼ teaspoon salt
½ cup unsalted butter,
   at room temperature
½ cup vegetable shortening
¾ cup granulated sugar
½ teaspoon vanilla extract
¼ cup dark molasses
⅓ cup finely chopped almonds
⅓ cup finely chopped crystallized ginger
   (optional)
½ cup turbinado sugar (see Note)

IN A BOWL, SIFT OR STIR TOGETHER THE FLOUR, BAKING SODA, 3 teaspoons cardamom, ginger, nutmeg, and salt. In a large bowl, beat the butter, shortening, and granulated sugar, using an electric mixer, until light and creamy. Beat in the vanilla. Stir the dry ingredients alternately with the molasses, beginning and ending with the dry ingredients, until well blended. Stir in the almonds and the crystallized ginger (if using).

Shape the dough into 2 logs, each 2 inches in diameter. Wrap each log in plastic wrap and chill for at least 2 hours. (When tightly sealed, the dough will keep for up to 1 week in the refrigerator. If the dough is wrapped in freezer-weight plastic bags or aluminum foil, it can be frozen for up to 6 months. To thaw, transfer the wrapped dough to the refrigerator for 2 hours before baking or let the wrapped dough stand at room temperature for 30 minutes.)

Preheat an oven to 350 degrees F. Position a rack in the center of the oven. Grease 2 baking sheets or line with parchment paper, and set aside.

In a small bowl, combine the remaining 1 teaspoon cardamom and the turbinado sugar. Place an 8-inch-wide piece of waxed paper on a work surface. Pour half of the sugar mixture down the center of the paper in a thick line as long as the cookie dough logs.

Remove 1 log from the refrigerator. Roll the log in the sugar mixture so that it coats the surface. With a sharp knife, cut in ¼-inch slices. Arrange the slices 1½ inches apart on the baking sheets. Bake until the cookies are golden brown, about 12 minutes.

Let the cookies cool on the baking sheet until firm before transferring to a wire rack to cool completely. Repeat with the second log. Store in an airtight container.

Note: Turbinado sugar is coarse, raw sugar that comes in large crystals. It can be found in the baking section of most supermarkets. If it is unavailable, granulated sugar can be substituted.

MAKES ABOUT 4 DOZEN COOKIES.

ABC Cookies

*S**ince the sixteenth century, gingerbread cookies have been cut in the shape of letters as a sweet way for children to learn the alphabet. In this recipe, you can roll the dough into ropes and shape them into letters. Little fingers will find this dough easy to manipulate; little mouths will find the cookies even easier to eat. For a tasty lesson in adding and subtracting, why not make numbers too?*

2 cups all-purpose flour
1/2 teaspoon baking soda
1/4 teaspoon salt
1 teaspoon ground ginger
1 teaspoon ground cinnamon
1/4 cup unsalted butter
1/2 cup firmly packed light brown sugar
1/2 cup light molasses
1 to 2 teaspoons milk, as needed

Icing
2 cups sifted powdered sugar
1/4 teaspoon vanilla extract
2 tablespoons milk, as needed
*Liquid food coloring for
    tinting (optional)*
Colored sugar for dusting

IN A LARGE BOWL, SIFT OR STIR TOGETHER THE FLOUR, BAKING soda, salt, ginger, and cinnamon. In a small saucepan, combine the butter, brown sugar, and molasses over low heat, stirring occasionally, until the butter melts and the mixture is blended. Remove from the heat and allow to cool to lukewarm. In a steady stream, pour the molasses mixture into the dry ingredients and add 1 to 2 teaspoons milk to make a firm dough. Gather the dough in a ball, wrap in waxed paper or plastic wrap, and chill for 2 hours or until firm. (When tightly sealed, the dough will keep for up to 1 week in the refrigerator. If the dough is wrapped in freezer-weight plastic bags or aluminum foil, it can be frozen for up to 6 months. To thaw, transfer the wrapped dough to the refrigerator for 2 hours before baking or let the wrapped dough stand at room temperature for 30 minutes to 1 hour.)

Preheat an oven to 350 degrees F. Position a rack in the center of the oven. Have ready 2 ungreased baking sheets.

Remove the dough from the refrigerator. Working as you would with clay, shape level tablespoonfuls of dough into ropes, 6 to 8 inches in length and 1/4 inch thick. Form into desired letters. The letter A, for example, is made with a 6-inch length creased in the middle. The horizontal piece is a 1-inch-long rope glued on with a drop of water. The letter C is made with a 6-inch curved length.

Bake until the cookies are set, about 10 minutes. Let the cookies cool on the sheets for 2 minutes before transferring to a wire rack to cool completely.

To make the icing, place the powdered sugar and vanilla in a small bowl. Stir in the milk, 1 teaspoon at a time, until it has a spreading consistency. You will have 1 cup of icing. To tint, divide the icing into 2 or 3 small bowls. Stir 1 or 2 drops of liquid food coloring into a bowl and blend until the desired color is reached.

Frost the cooled cookies with the icing, and sprinkle with the colored sugar.

Let the cookies dry on a wire rack until the icing is set, 20 to 30 minutes. Store in an airtight container, separating successive layers with sheets of waxed paper.

MAKES ABOUT 4 DOZEN COOKIES.

Chocolate-dipped Gingerbread Biscotti

[H]ere's a biscotti that combines the zest of crystallized ginger with the smooth, rich flavor of bittersweet chocolate. The trick to this spicy biscuit is to chop the crystallized ginger into both coarse and fine pieces. As the biscotti are baking, the finely chopped ginger seems to melt into the biscuits, imparting a spicy flavor, and the coarsely chopped pieces add a chewy bite to the finished cookies. Ken Hoyt, one of Oregon's talented interior designers, an ace in the kitchen, and a great pal, created this recipe as a gift for his many friends.

¾ cup crystallized ginger
2 tablespoons ground ginger
½ teaspoon ground allspice
½ teaspoon ground cinnamon
½ teaspoon ground nutmeg
½ cup granulated sugar
½ cup firmly packed dark brown sugar
6 tablespoons unsalted butter,
  at room temperature
2 large eggs
¼ cup light molasses
2¾ cups all-purpose flour
1½ teaspoons baking powder
⅔ cup (4 ounces) chopped
  bittersweet chocolate

DIVIDE THE CRYSTALLIZED GINGER INTO 2 EQUAL PORTIONS. Coarsely chop 1 portion and finely chop the other, and set aside.

In a large bowl, blend together the ground ginger, allspice, cinnamon, nutmeg, and granulated and brown sugars. In a large bowl, beat the butter with an electric mixer until light and creamy. Beat in the eggs, one at a time, followed by the molasses, until the mixture is smooth. Stir in both the coarsely chopped and the finely chopped ginger. Sift the flour and baking powder into the molasses mixture, and beat until just blended. The dough will be thick and slightly sticky. Divide the dough in half, wrap each half in waxed paper or plastic wrap, and chill for 2 to 3 hours. (When tightly sealed, the dough will keep for up to 1 week in the refrigerator.)

Preheat an oven to 375 degrees F. Position a rack in the center of the oven. Grease and flour a baking sheet or line with parchment paper, and set aside.

With lightly floured hands, shape each portion of dough into a loaf ½ inch thick, 2 inches wide, and 12 to 14 inches long. If your hands become sticky, wash, dry, and dust with flour again. Place the loaves on the prepared sheet at least 2 inches apart. Bake until the loaves are completely set and a toothpick inserted in the middle comes out clean, 25 to 30 minutes. Do not turn off the oven.

Place the baking sheet on a wire rack and let the loaves cool on the sheet for 5 minutes. Transfer the loaves to a cutting board and with a serrated knife, firmly cut each loaf on the diagonal into slices ½ inch thick. Place the slices upright on the baking sheet and return to the oven for 10 minutes, or longer if a crisper cookie is desired. Remove the biscotti from the oven and transfer to a wire rack to cool completely.

Melt the chocolate in a double boiler or in a microwave. With a spatula, spread the chocolate over half of each cookie. Set the cookies upright on a wire rack until the chocolate has set. Store in an airtight container, separating successive layers with sheets of waxed paper.

MAKES ABOUT 2½ DOZEN BISCOTTI.

Gingerbread Shortbread Bars

T hese sweet and wholesome cookie bars were created for people with food sensitivities by Julie Shivley, the owner of Soleil Natural Foods. Shivley founded her company when she discovered that her young daughter was sensitive to certain grains and food additives. The ingredients used in this recipe can be found at natural-food and health-food stores. The special note below lists the various substitutes that can be made for people allergic to certain ingredients.

2¼ cups organic whole wheat
  pastry flour
2 tablespoons toasted sesame seeds
  (see Note)
2 teaspoons ground ginger
1 teaspoon ground cinnamon
½ teaspoon nonaluminum
  baking powder
½ teaspoon sea salt
1 cup butter, softened
⅓ cup pure maple syrup
2 tablespoons sour cream

PREHEAT AN OVEN TO 350 DEGREES F. POSITION A RACK IN THE center of the oven. Grease a 9-by-12-inch baking pan, and set aside.

In a large bowl, combine the flour, the toasted sesame seeds (saving a pinch to sprinkle on top before baking), the ginger, cinnamon, baking powder, and sea salt. Add the butter and mix together with a fork or clean fingers until the mixture forms a coarse meal. Stir in the maple syrup and sour cream until well blended.

Spread the batter into the prepared pan. Bake until lightly browned, 25 to 30 minutes. Cool in the pan on a wire rack for 5 minutes before cutting into squares.

Note: To toast sesame seeds, place the seeds in a dry skillet over medium heat, stirring occasionally, until the seeds are light brown.

Variation: To frost the shortbread bars, dot the top of the just-baked shortbread with ¼ cup semisweet chocolate or carob chips. Frost the top of the shortbread as the chips melt. Cool and cut into squares.

MAKES 16 BARS.

Special Note: For those with wheat and lactose sensitivities, organic whole wheat pastry flour can be replaced in a one-to-one ratio with organic whole spelt, kamut, or teff flours. If the batter seems dry, add 1 to 2 tablespoons water as necessary. Clarified butter (ghee) can be used in place of butter in a one-to-one ratio. If you choose to frost the bars, dairy-free chocolate chips can be used in place of regular chocolate chips. Replace the sour cream with plain yogurt in a one-to-one ratio or leave out all together.

Five-spice Slippers

This unusual and delightful ginger-spiced shortbread uses Chinese five-spice powder, a blend of cinnamon, cloves, fennel seeds, star anise, and Szechwan peppercorns. For an elegant evening or an afternoon tea, dip the edges in semisweet chocolate laced with crystallized ginger. If you're in the mood for more ginger, you might like to accompany these cookies with a demitasse of qishr, an espresso-like coffee drink laced with ground ginger (recipe below).

½ cup (1 stick) unsalted butter
⅓ cup superfine sugar
1 cup all-purpose flour
1 teaspoon ground ginger
1 teaspoon Chinese five-spice powder
   (see Note)
¼ teaspoon salt
¼ cup coarsely chopped crystallized ginger

IN A BOWL, BEAT THE BUTTER AND SUGAR, USING AN ELECTRIC mixer, until light and fluffy. Sift the flour, ginger, Chinese five-spice powder, and salt into the butter mixture. With clean fingers or a wooden spoon, mix until the flour begins to disappear. Add the chopped crystallized ginger and continue to mix, gathering the dough up into a ball.

Line a baking sheet with parchment paper. Draw an 8-inch circle in the paper, using the base of a cake pan as the outline. Place the ball of dough in the center of the circle and roll out the dough to cover the circle. If an even edge is desired, use a sharp knife to cut around the outline of the circle, discarding any leftover dough. Or, place dough in an ungreased 8-inch round cake pan with a removable bottom, and press it firmly into the pan. Score the dough into 8 wedges. Cover with plastic wrap and chill for 1 hour.

Preheat an oven to 325 degrees F. Position a rack in the center of the oven. Bake until the shortbread begins to color, 25 to 30 minutes. Remove from the oven and, with a sharp knife, cut the scores to make 8 wedges and cool on the baking sheet or in the pan for 5 minutes. Gently remove with a spatula, and transfer to a wire rack to cool completely. Store in an airtight container.

Note: Chinese five-spice powder can be found in most supermarket spice sections and in Asian grocery stores. One familiar brand is Spice Islands.

Variation: To make Chocolate Velvet Slippers, melt 3 ounces of chopped, semisweet chocolate in the top of a double boiler and dip the rounded edge of each cookie into the warm chocolate. Lay the cookies on a wire rack. Press slivers of crystallized ginger onto the cooling chocolate and allow the chocolate to set at room temperature.

MAKES 8 WEDGES.

Recipe for qishr: Pour 1 cup cold water into a saucepan. Add 1 tablespoon ground espresso-roast coffee beans, 1 tablespoon granulated sugar, and 1¼ teaspoons ground ginger. Bring the mixture to a rolling boil. Remove from the heat until the bubbling stops. Repeat two more times. After the third boil, let the mixture steep for 2 minutes. Pour slowly into 2 demitasse cups. Part of the drink's exotic romance is serving it unstrained.

Gingerbread Desserts and Cakes

Peekaboo Cupcakes

or a backyard picnic or a children's birthday party, these gingerbread cupcakes have all the right ingredients—a scrumptious cake, a yummy frosting, and a crisp cookie to nibble.

Cupcakes
1¼ cups all-purpose flour
2 teaspoons ground ginger
1 teaspoon ground cinnamon
½ teaspoon ground cloves
¼ cup unsalted butter, at room temperature
¼ cup firmly packed light brown sugar
¾ cup light molasses
1 large egg, lightly beaten
1 teaspoon baking soda
½ cup boiling water

Sweet Citrus Icing
¼ cup unsalted butter, softened
½ teaspoon vanilla extract
1 teaspoon grated orange zest
Pinch of salt
1½ cups sifted powdered sugar
2 teaspoons freshly squeezed lemon juice

12 Gingerbread Men cookies (page 38)
Colored sprinkles and tiny gumdrops
  for garnish (optional)

TO MAKE THE CUPCAKES, PREHEAT AN OVEN TO 350 DEGREES F. Position a rack in the center of the oven. Grease 12 standard muffin cups or line with paper liners, and set aside.

In a bowl, sift or stir together the flour, ginger, cinnamon, and cloves. In a large bowl, blend together the butter, brown sugar, and molasses. Stir in the egg. In a small bowl, dissolve the baking soda in the boiling water. The mixture will be foamy. Stir in the dry ingredients alternately with the boiling water, beginning and ending with the dry ingredients, until thoroughly blended.

Spoon the batter into the prepared muffin cups, filling each two-thirds full. Bake until a toothpick inserted in the middle comes out clean, about 20 minutes. Let cool in the pan on a wire rack for 5 minutes. Cool thoroughly before frosting.

To make the icing, beat the butter, vanilla, orange zest, and salt in a small bowl, using an electric mixer, until light and fluffy. Gradually beat in the powdered sugar and lemon juice until well blended.

Spread the icing on the cupcakes. Gently insert a gingerbread cookie in the center of each cupcake so that the cookie figure appears to be peeking out of the frosting. When using a large cookie, you'll find it easier to cut the cookie in half or in sections so that it does not need to be as deeply inserted. Decorate the frosting with sprinkles or gumdrops, if desired.

MAKES 12 CUPCAKES.

Brandy Snaps with Warm Lemon Curd, Raspberries, and Mascarpone Cream

*T**his delectable dessert combines several luscious flavors and textures in one gorgeous creation. The cookies take a bit of practice to make, but once you have the technique down, it's simple. You can always break your mistakes into shards, dip the edges in melted semisweet chocolate, and serve alongside the completed dessert.*

½ cup sifted all-purpose flour
⅓ cup granulated sugar
2 tablespoons ground ginger
¼ cup light or dark molasses
1 tablespoon brandy
¼ cup unsalted butter
1 cup Mascarpone Cream (page 72)
5 cups fresh raspberries
2 cups warm purchased lemon curd or homemade Lemon Curd (page 74)

PREHEAT AN OVEN TO 350 DEGREES F. POSITION A RACK IN the center of the oven. Line a baking sheet with aluminum foil, grease the foil, and set aside.

In a bowl, sift the flour again with the sugar and ginger. In a large, heavy saucepan, bring the molasses and brandy to a boil. Boil for 1 minute, maintaining frothy bubbles while stirring. Remove from the heat and add the butter, stirring until it has melted. Let the mixture cool slightly, then gradually add the dry ingredients, stirring until completely blended.

Drop the mixture by tablespoonfuls 2 ½ to 3 inches apart on the prepared baking sheet. Bake only 4 cookies at a time; there should be enough dough for about 12 cookies. Bake for 12 to 15 minutes. In testing the cookies for doneness, color and texture are important: the dough needs to be spread thin and bubbling; it also needs to be a slightly chocolate-caramel color. You may think they are just about to burn. Remove from the oven and let the cookies cool in the pan a little more than 1 minute, until they can be easily handled but are still warm to the touch.

To shape the cookies, set each one inside a small soup bowl. Make extra cookie bowls in case of breakage. Extra cookies can also be shaped into tubes, by rolling each one around the handle of a wooden spoon and placing on a wire rack covered with parchment paper to cool. If the cookies harden on the baking sheet before shaping, reheat them in the oven for about 1 minute or until softened. To retain their crispness, these cookies are best made on the day they are to be served. If necessary, they can be stored in an airtight container for up to 3 days.

To assemble the dessert, place a dollop of Mascarpone Cream in the center of each dessert plate. Secure a brandy snap to the plate by pressing it onto the cream. Fill the snap with ½ cup raspberries.

Spoon ¼ cup of the warm Lemon Curd over the berries. Garnish with additional raspberries and chilled Mascarpone Cream. Repeat with the remaining snaps.

SERVES 8.

Chocolate–Sour Cream Gingerbread

No one loves chocolate more than Robert Hammond, the creative chef behind Moonstruck Chocolatier. His lavish candies and exquisite truffles can be found in chocolate shops and gourmet stops from California to New York, but his heart, his home, and his chocolate gingerbread have stayed in Oregon. That is, until now. Here's Robert's recipe for his favorite gingerbread.

1/3 cup vegetable shortening,
    cut into small pieces
1 cup granulated sugar
2 large eggs, at room temperature
1 cup sour cream, at room temperature
1/2 cup light molasses
1 3/4 cups all-purpose flour
1/4 cup unsweetened cocoa
1 1/2 teaspoons ground ginger
1 teaspoon ground cinnamon
1/4 teaspoon ground cloves
1 teaspoon baking soda
1/2 teaspoon salt

Icing
1 cup sifted powdered sugar
1 tablespoon milk or water

PREHEAT AN OVEN TO 350 DEGREES F. POSITION A RACK IN THE center of the oven. Lightly grease a 13-by-9-by-2-inch cake pan and set aside.

To make the gingerbread, in a large bowl, beat together the shortening and sugar, using an electric mixer, until light and creamy. Beat in the eggs, one egg at a time, until well blended. Stir in the sour cream and molasses. Sift the flour, cocoa, ginger, cinnamon, cloves, baking soda, and salt into the molasses mixture, and gently fold in. Pour into the prepared pan. Bake until a toothpick inserted in the middle comes out clean, 35 to 40 minutes. Cool in the pan on a wire rack.

To make the icing, in a small bowl, whisk the powdered sugar and milk until blended. Brush the icing over the top of the cake.

Variation: To make Chocolate-Frosted Sour-Cream Gingerbread Cupcakes, divide the batter among 12 greased or paper-lined muffin cups. Bake for 20 minutes. To frost, melt 4 ounces premium semisweet chocolate and brush on top of the cupcakes.

SERVES 6 TO 8.

Lemon-Strawberry Tartlets

ere's an easy way to make individual desserts for family and friends. Children love to help make these rustic tartlets. The tartlet shells can also be used to make other quick and tasty desserts by using simple fillings such as a small scoop of ice cream or frozen yogurt topped with fresh fruit, sundae syrups, or any of the Gingerbread Accompaniments (pages 69–79).

Tartlets
1/4 cup unsalted butter, cut into
    small pieces
3 tablespoons firmly packed brown sugar
2 tablespoons dark molasses
1 large egg
1 1/2 cups all-purpose flour
1/4 teaspoon salt
1 teaspoon ground ginger
1/2 teaspoon ground cinnamon
1/2 teaspoon ground allspice

Filling
3/4 cup purchased lemon curd or
    homemade Lemon Curd (page 74)
3/4 cup plain or lemon-flavored yogurt
1 1/2 cups small, fresh strawberries,
    hulled and halved

TO MAKE THE TARTLETS, IN A LARGE BOWL, BEAT TOGETHER THE butter and brown sugar, using an electric mixer, until light and creamy. Beat in the molasses and egg. Sift the flour, salt, ginger, cinnamon, and allspice into the molasses mixture, and beat until well blended. The dough will be sticky. Cover and chill the dough for 1 hour.

Preheat an oven to 350 degrees F. Position a rack in the center of the oven. Invert a standard muffin tin and grease the outside of 10 muffin cups.

Separate the dough into 2 balls, leaving 1 ball covered in the refrigerator. On a lightly floured work surface, roll out the ball to a 1/8 inch thickness. Cut the dough with a 4-inch round or fluted biscuit cutter. With a spatula, lift each round and place on top of the prepared muffin cup. Using clean fingers, form the dough into a tartlet shell by pleating it to fit against the outside of the cup. Repeat until all the dough is used. Prick each tartlet shell with the tines of a fork.

Bake until the shells are firm to the touch, 12 to 14 minutes. Let the shells rest on the pan for 2 minutes before removing them to a wire rack to cool completely.

To make the filling, in a bowl, combine the lemon curd and yogurt until well blended.

To assemble the tartlets, place 2 heaping tablespoons of the lemon curd mixture into each tartlet shell. Arrange as many sliced berries as possible on top of the filling, sliced side down.

Variation: To reduce the fat, substitute low-fat lemon yogurt for the lemon curd.

MAKES 10 TARTLETS.

Carrot-Ginger Cake with Burnt Sugar Icing and Caramel Wisps

*I*f you like carrot cake, you'll love this gingerbread rendition.

Carrot-Ginger Cake
3½ cups all-purpose flour
1 tablespoon ground ginger
2 teaspoons ground cinnamon
1 teaspoon ground nutmeg
2 teaspoons baking soda
½ teaspoon baking powder
1 teaspoon salt
⅔ cup unsalted butter, cut into
    small pieces
½ cup firmly packed light
    brown sugar
1½ cups light molasses
2 large eggs
2 tablespoons grated orange zest
⅔ cup freshly squeezed orange juice
½ cup hot water
2 cups shredded carrots

Burnt Sugar Icing
½ cup granulated sugar
¼ cup boiling water
1½ cups sifted powdered sugar
Pinch of salt
4 ounces cream cheese, at room
    temperature
3 tablespoons unsalted butter,
    at room temperature
2 teaspoons molasses

Caramel Wisps
1 cup granulated sugar
2 tablespoons water

To make the cake, preheat an oven to 350 degrees F. Position a rack in the center of the oven. Grease and flour two 9-inch round cake pans. Line the bottom of each pan with parchment or waxed paper, butter the paper, and set aside.

In a bowl, sift or stir together the flour, ginger, cinnamon, nutmeg, baking soda, baking powder, and salt. In a large bowl, whip the butter and sugar, using an electric mixer, until light and fluffy. Beat in the molasses and eggs. Stir in the orange zest and juice until blended. Add the dry ingredients alternately with the hot water, beginning and ending with the dry ingredients, until well blended. Stir in the shredded carrots.

Pour the batter into the prepared pans and smooth out with a knife. Bake until a toothpick inserted in the middle comes out clean, 40 to 45 minutes. Remove from the oven and run a knife around the edge of each pan. Cool the cakes in the pans for 10 minutes on a wire rack. Invert each cake, remove the paper, and let cool completely on a wire rack. (The layers can be made ahead of time, wrapped in plastic wrap and aluminum foil, and frozen for up to 2 weeks.)

To make the icing, cook the granulated sugar in a small, heavy saucepan over medium-high heat, stirring constantly, until the sugar melts and turns a deep caramel color (there will be lumps). Remove from the heat and carefully stir in the boiling water. To avoid splatters, pour the water along the side of the skillet. Continue to stir until the mixture is well blended. Cool to room temperature.

Sift the powdered sugar and salt into a small bowl. In a bowl, beat the cream cheese and butter, using an electric mixer, until light and fluffy. Beat in the molasses until combined. Drizzle 1 tablespoon of the sugar syrup into the butter mixture and beat until combined. Alternately add the powdered sugar and drizzle in the sugar syrup, beating constantly, until the frosting is smooth. Cover and chill for 1 hour. (The icing can be made ahead and refrigerated. For best results, use within 3 days.)

To make the caramel wisps, lightly coat a baking sheet with vegetable oil. In a small saucepan, combine the granulated sugar and water and let the mixture stand for 10 minutes. Over low heat, stir the mixture until the sugar dissolves. With a pastry brush dipped in hot water, wash down any grains of sugar on the sides of the pan. Increase the heat and bring the liquid to a vigorous boil. Stop stirring. Place a candy thermometer in the pan and boil until the thermometer reaches 345 degrees F.

Using a spoon, drizzle a thin stream of caramel across the prepared baking sheet. Be very careful—the sugar syrup is extremely hot. Continue by making delicate crisscross lines across the sheet. The finer the lines, the more delicate the wisps will be. Let the caramel cool, then lift it gently from the sheet, breaking the wisps into large pieces. Store in an airtight container for up to 2 days before using.

To assemble the cake, place 1 tablespoon of the icing in the center of a serving plate. Set one layer, flat side up, on the plate, pressing slightly to secure the layer to the icing. Spread half of the icing over the first layer. Place the second layer, top side up, over the frosted layer, and spread with the remaining icing.

If serving the cake immediately, place the caramel wisps upright in a circular pattern around the top of the cake. If serving the cake in several hours or the next day, tent the cake with aluminum foil and refrigerate. Bring the cake to room temperature before decorating with the caramel wisps.

SERVES 10 TO 12.

Peach-Blueberry Crisp

This is one of those desserts for people who love blueberries and peaches. These luscious summer fruits are the vehicles for a dynamite gingersnap crisp. There's plenty of crunchy topping because my family eats it like cookie dough, so we always have to make extra.

4 large ripe peaches
3 cups fresh blueberries
Zest of 1 small lemon or orange
$\frac{1}{3}$ cup granulated sugar
2 tablespoons quick-cooking tapioca
   or cornstarch
$\frac{3}{4}$ cup all-purpose flour
$\frac{1}{2}$ cup firmly packed light brown sugar
1 teaspoon ground ginger
1 teaspoon ground cinnamon
$\frac{1}{4}$ teaspoon salt
$\frac{1}{2}$ cup finely chopped toasted pecans
   (see Note)
6 tablespoons unsalted butter,
   cut into small pieces
1 cup coarsely broken purchased
   gingersnap cookies

Sweetened Whipped Cream (page 71)
   or 2 cups (1 pint) vanilla ice cream

PREHEAT AN OVEN TO 350 DEGREES F. POSITION A RACK IN the center of the oven. Grease an 8-inch-square baking dish.

To peel the peaches, bring a large pot of water to a boil. Cut a shallow X in the bottom of each peach and place the peaches into the boiling water for 30 seconds. Immediately immerse them in a bowl of cold water and drain. The peels will slip right off. Slice the peaches into $\frac{1}{4}$-inch-thick slices and place in a large bowl. Wash and pick over the blueberries and add to the peaches. Lightly toss the fruit with the citrus zest, sugar, and tapioca or cornstarch. Transfer to the baking dish.

In a bowl, stir together the flour, brown sugar, ginger, cinnamon, and salt. Stir in the pecans. Add the butter and mix together with a fork or clean fingers until crumbly. Stir in the gingersnap crumbs. Generously sprinkle over the top of the fruit mixture. There will be leftover topping.

Bake until the top is lightly browned and the fruit is bubbling, about 35 minutes. Cool slightly on a wire rack. Serve warm with Sweetened Whipped Cream or vanilla ice cream.

Note: To toast pecans, spread shelled nuts in a shallow pan. Toast in an oven preheated to 350 degrees F, stirring occasionally, until lightly browned, 8 to 10 minutes.

SERVES 6 TO 8.

Crystallized Ginger and Apple Tarte Tatin

A tarte Tatin is simply a glorious upside-down cake. It originated more than a hundred years ago at the Lamotte-Beuvron restaurant on the Loire River in France. This crystallized ginger rendition with its honey-sweetened crust was created by pastry chef Jennifer Flannigan for Paley's Place, a much-celebrated restaurant in Portland, Oregon.

Pastry
1 cup all-purpose flour
Pinch of salt
1 teaspoon ground ginger
$^1/_2$ teaspoon ground cinnamon
$^1/_4$ teaspoon ground nutmeg
Pinch of ground cloves
3 tablespoons granulated sugar
4 tablespoons chilled unsalted butter,
    cut into small pieces
$^1/_4$ cup toasted and ground walnuts
    (see Note)
2 teaspoons honey
1 tablespoon ice water

Apple Filling
5 or 6 tart apples such as Granny Smith
    or Newton
Juice and zest of 1 lemon
$1^1/_2$ cups granulated sugar
$^3/_4$ cup unsalted butter
3 ounces crystallized ginger,
    coarsely chopped

Sweetened Whipped Cream (page 71)

To make the pastry, in a large bowl, sift or stir together the flour, salt, ginger, cinnamon, nutmeg, cloves, and sugar. With a pastry blender or 2 knives, cut in the butter until the mixture looks like cornmeal. Stir in the walnuts. Add the honey and toss lightly with a fork until blended. Add the ice water, 1 teaspoon at a time, until the dough holds together and can be shaped into a ball. Wrap the dough in plastic wrap and chill for at least 1 hour.

To prepare the filling, peel and core the apples. Slice each apple into eighths and place in a bowl. As you cut the apples, drizzle some of the lemon juice over them to keep them from discoloring. Add the lemon zest and $^1/_2$ cup sugar, toss to combine, and let the mixture rest for 20 minutes. You will notice the apples begin to release their juice.

In an 8-inch skillet, melt the butter over medium to medium-high heat. Add the remaining 1 cup sugar to the butter. Stir until the liquid bubbles slightly and turns caramel brown. Remove from the heat.

Drain the apple slices and arrange in a circular pattern in the bottom of the skillet. Be careful not to burn your fingers since the caramel sauce is hot. Tuck some of the chopped crystallized ginger among the apple slices. Top with the remaining apple slices to fill the pan, and tuck in the remaining chopped ginger.

Preheat an oven to 450 degrees F. Position a rack in the lower middle level of the oven.

Place the skillet over medium-high heat, pressing the apples down with a spoon. Draw off the juices with a bulb baster and drip over the apples. When the apples begin to soften, cover the skillet with aluminum foil, and reduce the heat to medium. Cook for 10 to 15 minutes, basting frequently. The juice will thicken. Remove from the heat.

Remove the dough from the refrigerator. On a lightly floured surface, roll out the chilled dough into a circle $^3/_{16}$ inch thick and 1 inch larger than the skillet. Lay the dough over the apples, pressing the edges along the inside of the pan. With a paring knife, make several steam vents in the dough.

Bake until the pastry has browned, about 20 minutes. The pan and the handle are hot, so be sure to use oven mitts when removing the skillet from the oven. Check the consistency of the juice. If it is too runny, briefly place the skillet over medium-high heat to reduce the juice. Be careful—you don't want the juices to evaporate.

To unmold the tart, place a serving plate over the skillet as you would a lid and invert. Rearrange any apple slices that have slipped. Serve warm or cold with Sweetened Whipped Cream.

Note: To toast and grind walnuts, spread shelled nuts in a shallow pan. Toast in an oven preheated to 350 degrees F, stirring occasionally, until lightly browned, 5 to 7 minutes. Use a food processor or blender to grind nuts to desired texture. Use quick on/off pulses. Do not overprocess or the nuts will become nut butter.

SERVES 6.

Pumpkin Gingersnap Cheesecake

*S*ilky rich and deliciously creamy, this festive cheesecake with its crunchy walnut brittle topping is a delicious make-ahead dessert to serve during the holidays. Pastry chef Jennifer Flannagan devised this delightful cheesecake with its candylike topping.

Crust
1/2 cup graham cracker crumbs
3/4 cup gingersnap crumbs
2 1/2 tablespoons granulated sugar
1 teaspoon ground ginger
1/4 cup unsalted butter, melted
1 egg white, well beaten

Filling
2 cups (16 ounces) cream cheese
1 cup sour cream
1/2 cup firmly packed brown sugar
1/2 cup granulated sugar
4 large eggs, separated
1 cup plus 1 tablespoon canned
    unsweetened pumpkin purée
2 teaspoons vanilla extract
3 tablespoons cornstarch
1 teaspoon ground ginger
1/2 teaspoon ground cinnamon
Pinch of ground nutmeg
Pinch of ground cloves

Topping
2/3 cup coarsely chopped toasted walnuts
    (see Note)
2 teaspoons ground ginger
1/2 cup firmly packed brown sugar
1 1/2 tablespoons unsalted butter,
    cut into small pieces

PREHEAT AN OVEN TO 375 DEGREES F. POSITION A RACK IN the center of the oven. Position a second rack directly below it.

To make the crust, in a large bowl, combine the graham cracker and gingersnap crumbs, sugar, and ginger. Stir in the melted butter. Firmly press the crumbs into the bottom of a 9 1/2-inch springform pan. Brush the crust lightly with the egg white and chill for at least 15 minutes before filling and baking.

To make the filling, in a large bowl, beat together the cream cheese, sour cream, and brown and granulated sugars, using an electric mixer, until smooth. Gently beat in the egg yolks, then the pumpkin purée, vanilla, cornstarch, ginger, cinnamon, nutmeg, and cloves. In a large bowl, beat the egg whites, with a whisk or an electric mixer, until stiff peaks are formed. Fold the egg whites into the cream cheese mixture.

Pour the filling into the prepared pan and place in the oven. Set an 8-inch-square baking pan filled halfway with hot water on the rack below the cheesecake (this helps prevent the top of the cheesecake from cracking). Bake until the center does not tremble when the cake is gently shaken, about 1 1/2 hours.

Remove from the oven and allow to cool for several minutes. Place a rack 4 to 5 inches from the heat source of a broiler. Preheat the broiler.

To make the topping, in a small bowl, combine the walnuts, ginger, and sugar. Add the butter and mix together with a fork or clean fingers until crumbly. Sprinkle over the warm cheesecake and place in the broiler to melt the sugar and caramelize the topping, 30 to 40 seconds. Watch carefully so that the topping does not burn.

Remove the cheesecake from the broiler and let cool to room temperature. Cover and chill for at least 6 hours or as long as overnight. When it is chilled, run a knife around the edge of the cheesecake and remove the pan rim. Set the cheesecake on a serving plate without removing the pan bottom.

Note: To toast walnuts, spread shelled nuts in a shallow pan. Toast in an oven preheated to 350 degrees F, stirring occasionally, until lightly browned, 8 to 10 minutes.

SERVES 10.

Gingerbread Cookie–Ice Cream Sandwiches

Crisp and creamy—there is something positively paradoxical, but absolutely right about an ice-cream sandwich. In this recipe, the fresh ginger ice cream has a peppery zing that guests find ravishing. This dessert is a favorite at our house when friends come over for a summer barbecue. I often make a variety of ice-cream fillings. Several quick-to-fix recipes in this book are scrumptious when sandwiched between two soft molasses cookies: Val's Molasses Ice Cream (page 78), Cinnamon Ice Cream (page 78), and Ginger–Lemon Ice Cream (page 79).

Cookies
$\frac{1}{2}$ cup plus 2 tablespoons unsalted butter, cut into pieces
$\frac{2}{3}$ cup granulated sugar
$\frac{1}{3}$ cup firmly packed light or dark brown sugar
$\frac{1}{4}$ cup light or dark molasses
1 large egg
2 cups all-purpose flour
1 teaspoon baking soda
Pinch of salt
$1\frac{1}{2}$ teaspoons ground ginger
1 teaspoon ground cinnamon
$\frac{1}{4}$ teaspoon ground nutmeg

Ice Cream
4 cups half-and-half
1 cup granulated sugar
$\frac{1}{4}$ cup grated fresh ginger
6 large egg yolks

PREHEAT AN OVEN TO 350 DEGREES F. POSITION A RACK IN the center of the oven. Grease a baking sheet or line with parchment paper, and set aside.

To make the cookies, in a large bowl, beat together the butter, $\frac{1}{3}$ cup granulated sugar, and brown sugar, using an electric mixer, until light and creamy. Beat in the molasses and egg until well blended. Sift the flour, baking soda, salt, ginger, cinnamon, and nutmeg into the molasses mixture, and beat until well blended.

With clean hands, form balls $1\frac{1}{2}$ inches in diameter (the size of large walnuts). Roll each ball in a bowl filled with the remaining $\frac{1}{3}$ cup granulated sugar. Place the dough balls 4 inches apart on the prepared sheet. With the bottom of a custard cup or small bowl, flatten each ball into a 2-inch disk. Bake until the cookies are firm to the touch, about 12 minutes. Let the cookies cool slightly on the sheet before transferring to a wire rack to cool completely. Repeat with remaining dough. You should have about 32 cookies. Store or freeze the cookies in an airtight container at room temperature or in a freezer until ready to use.

To make the ice cream, in a saucepan, combine the half-and-half and sugar over medium-high heat and scald (bring almost a boil). Remove from the heat and let the half-and-half cool to nearly room temperature; otherwise, when the fresh ginger is added, the liquid may curdle. Stir in the grated ginger, cover, and allow to steep overnight in the refrigerator. Remove from the refrigerator and strain the liquid through a fine-mesh sieve. Discard the grated ginger.

In a large bowl, whisk the egg yolks until light yellow. Slowly whisk in the half-and-half. Pour the liquid into the top of a double boiler. Cook over water that has been brought to a boil and reduced to medium, stirring constantly with a wooden spoon, until the custard thickens and covers the back of the spoon, about 10 minutes. Strain the custard through a fine-mesh sieve into a container. Cover with plastic wrap and refrigerate until thoroughly chilled, at least 3 hours or as long as overnight.

Place the mixture in an ice-cream maker and freeze according to the manufacturer's instructions. Transfer the ice cream to a container, cover, and freeze for several hours.

To assemble the sandwiches, place 16 cookies upside down on a baking sheet lined with parchment or waxed paper. Scoop $\frac{1}{4}$ cup ice cream and set on top of each cookie. Place a cookie, bottom side down, on top of each ice-cream mound and gently press it down. Place the sandwiches on a baking sheet in the freezer for 1 hour.

Remove the sandwiches from the freezer. If you wish, trim any excess ice cream with a paring knife. Wrap each sandwich in plastic wrap and return to the freezer. The sandwiches are best eaten within 3 days.

MAKES 16 SANDWICHES.

Indian Gingerbread Pudding with Autumn Compote

This satisfying and delicious bread pudding with its pear and cranberry compote is comfort food at its best. Made with hearty polenta, real maple syrup, and warm gingerbread spices, it is a wonderful autumn or winter dessert. Slow baking makes this a creamy pudding, delicately infused with flavors. This recipe is another creation of Jennifer Flannagan, pastry chef at Paley's Place.

Pudding
2 cups milk
Pinch of salt
1/2 cup stone-ground polenta
   (yellow cornmeal)
1/4 cup firmly packed dark brown sugar
1/2 cup whipping cream
1/3 cup maple syrup
1 teaspoon ground ginger
1/2 teaspoon ground cinnamon
1/4 teaspoon ground nutmeg

Compote
1/2 lemon
2 large, ripe pears such as Comice,
   Bartlett, or Bosc, peeled, cored,
   and diced
1/4 to 1/2 cup dried cranberries
1/2 cup firmly packed brown sugar or
   maple sugar granules
1 teaspoon ground ginger

PREHEAT AN OVEN TO 275 DEGREES F. POSITION A RACK IN the center of the oven. Place a baking sheet on the rack. Butter six 6-ounce ramekins or custard cups.

In a large saucepan, heat the milk and salt over medium heat until almost boiling. Slowly whisk in the polenta, and stir constantly until the polenta thickens like oatmeal and absorbs most of the milk, about 10 minutes. Remove from heat and stir in the brown sugar, cream, maple syrup, ginger, cinnamon, and nutmeg. Fill each prepared ramekin with 3/4 cup of the polenta mixture. Cover each ramekin with an aluminum foil cap, and place on the baking sheet so that the ramekins are not touching. Bake for 1 1/2 to 2 hours (1 1/2 hours will give the pudding a creamy texture, 2 hours a firmer consistency). Remove from the oven and serve warm or at room temperature.

To make the compote, remove the zest from the lemon half. Squeeze the juice from the lemon. In a saucepan, combine the lemon zest and juice, pears, cranberries, brown sugar or maple sugar granules, and ginger. Toss gently until well mixed. Heat gently over medium heat until the fruit begins to release its juice and the cranberries plump. Serve warm over the bread pudding.

SERVES 6.

Gingerbread Accompaniments

Decorative Icing

To dress up and trim cutout cookies, this uncooked icing is simple to make. Unlike granulated sugar, powdered sugar dissolves easily without cooking and makes a smooth finish. If you wish to flavor the icing, the vanilla extract can be substituted with other extracts or even strong black coffee.

2 tablespoons unsalted butter, softened
2 cups powdered sugar, sifted
2 tablespoons whipping cream,
  or as needed
½ teaspoon vanilla extract
Liquid food coloring (optional)

IN A LARGE BOWL, BEAT THE BUTTER WITH AN ELECTRIC MIXER until light and creamy. Gradually beat in the powdered sugar. Blend in the cream and vanilla until the icing is smooth and creamy. To thin, stir in additional whipping cream, 1 teaspoon at a time. If not using the icing immediately, cover and refrigerate for up to 3 days.

To tint the icing, divide into 2 or 3 small bowls. Stir 1 or 2 drops of liquid food coloring into each bowl and blend until the desired color is reached.

MAKES ABOUT 2 CUPS.

Sweetened Whipped Cream

Most cookbooks don't bother explaining how to make whipped cream. This is too bad, because there are certain steps you can take that will guarantee a long-lasting, delectable topping. ✤ *You want to use heavy whipping cream. Avoid ultra-pasteurized cream because the high heat required for this process breaks down the fat, which contributes to the volume. Chilling makes whipping go faster. If you are whisking by hand, chill the whisk, or if you are using an electric mixer, chill the beaters. In either case, make sure your bowl is made from stainless steel, glass, or ceramic, and chill it as well. Aluminum can give the cream a gray tinge; plastic cannot be chilled thoroughly.* ✤ *When whipped cream is the delicious crown for a homemade dessert, I like to whip it by hand because this allows more air to be incorporated into the luscious topping.*

1 cup chilled whipping cream
2 tablespoons granulated sugar
1 teaspoon vanilla

IN A CHILLED BOWL, WHISK THE CREAM WITH A CHILLED WHISK or beat with the chilled beaters of an electric mixer until the cream begins to thicken. Add the sugar and vanilla and continue to whip until soft peaks are formed. Cover the bowl with plastic wrap, and chill until ready to use. For best results, use within 8 hours.

Variation: To make flavored creams, add one of the following flavorings with the sugar and vanilla: ³⁄₄ teaspoon ground ginger, ¹⁄₂ teaspoon ground cinnamon, 1 tablespoon cognac, or 1 tablespoon sherry. You can also substitute your favorite spice or flavored syrup.

MAKES ABOUT 2 CUPS.

Mascarpone Cream

Mascarpone is a fresh, Italian dessert cheese with a soft, delicate flavor. It's available wherever you find fine cheeses. When you combine it with sweetened whipping cream, it becomes a buttery-rich accent for any dessert.

1 cup chilled whipping cream
1/4 cup granulated sugar
1/2 teaspoon vanilla extract (optional)
1 cup (1/2 pound) mascarpone cheese

IN A CHILLED BOWL, WHISK THE CREAM BRIEFLY UNTIL IT BEGINS to thicken. Add the sugar and the vanilla (if using), and continue to whip until thick peaks form.

In a large bowl, whip the mascarpone cheese, using an electric mixer, until light and creamy. Blend one-third of the whipped cream into the mascarpone. Fold in the remaining whipped cream. Cover and chill before serving. For best quality, use within 3 days.

MAKES ABOUT 3 CUPS.

Honey Cream

This simple sauce beckons us with memories of warm summer days and fresh, ripe fruits. It's divine with any gingerbread and fruit medley. Be sure to use a very good quality honey, the kind you find at a farmer's market.

3/4 cup whipping cream
1/2 cup honey
2 tablespoons unsalted butter,
cut into small pieces

IN A SMALL, HEAVY SAUCEPAN, COMBINE THE WHIPPING CREAM, honey, and unsalted butter. Place over low heat, and stir until the butter melts and the ingredients are blended. Remove from the heat and cool. Refrigerate the cream until it thickens, 2 to 3 hours. For best quality, use within 3 days.

MAKES 1 1/3 CUPS.

Maple Cream

A hint of maple flavoring makes this an exquisite autumn topping on any kind of gingerbread.

1 cup chilled whipping cream
1½ tablespoons pure maple syrup,
    at room temperature

IN A CHILLED BOWL, WHISK THE CREAM UNTIL IT JUST BEGINS to form soft peaks. Drizzle in the maple syrup, continuing to whisk until soft peaks form and begin to hold their shape. Cover and chill until ready to use.

MAKES ABOUT 2 CUPS.

Golden Pear Compote

This medley of fresh pears, golden raisins, and cranberries makes a delicious alternative to maple syrup. It's delicious on warm gingerbread and vanilla ice cream. Sometimes I like to vary the dried fruit used in this compote. For the cranberries, I'll substitute diced, dried apples or peaches. To add extra zing, toss in some chopped crystallized ginger.

½ cup granulated sugar
2½ teaspoons cornstarch
1 cup apple juice
¼ cup firmly packed light
    brown sugar
1 tablespoon minced orange zest
½ teaspoon ground ginger
¼ teaspoon ground cloves
⅓ cup golden raisins
¼ cup dried cranberries (optional)
4 large, ripe pears such as
    Bosc or Anjou

PREHEAT AN OVEN TO 350 DEGREES F. POSITION A RACK IN the center of the oven.

In a saucepan, blend together the granulated sugar and cornstarch. Add the apple juice, brown sugar, orange zest, ginger, cloves, raisins, and cranberries (if using). Simmer over medium heat, stirring occasionally, until the sugars dissolve.

Peel and core the pears, then cut lengthwise into eighths. Place in a shallow oven-proof baking dish so that the slices are nestled and all touch the bottom. Pour the apple juice mixture over the pears. Bake until the pears are tender, about 30 minutes, basting them several times. Serve warm or let cool to room temperature. To store, place in a covered container in the refrigerator. For best quality, use within 3 days.

MAKES 2½ TO 3 CUPS; SERVES 4 TO 6.

Orange-Honey Butter

A satisfying spread for scones and muffins, this orange-scented honey butter melts delicately and deliciously over waffles and pancakes. For a variation, try adding your favorite toasted nuts.

½ cup unsalted butter, softened
1 tablespoon minced orange zest
¼ cup honey

IN A BOWL, CREAM THE BUTTER AND ORANGE ZEST UNTIL the butter is light and fluffy. Beat in the honey until well combined. Cover and refrigerate to let the flavors infuse, 2 to 3 hours. Bring to room temperature before serving. Cover any leftover butter with plastic wrap and refrigerate. For best quality, use within 1 week.

Variation: To make Honey-Nut Orange Butter, stir in ¼ cup finely chopped toasted pecans or toasted almonds after the honey. To toast pecans or almonds, spread shelled nuts in a shallow pan. Toast in an oven preheated to 350 degrees F, stirring occasionally, until lightly browned, 8 to 10 minutes.

MAKES ¾ CUP.

Lemon Curd

This creamy lemon curd is used warm as a sauce or chilled as a filling for cakes and tarts, and as a spread for toast and cookies. Some people like it by the spoonful at midnight.

4 large lemons
4 large eggs
¾ cup granulated sugar
1 cup (2 sticks) plus 2 tablespoons
    unsalted butter, melted

REMOVE THE ZEST FROM THE LEMONS, BEING CAREFUL NOT to include any white pith. Squeeze the juice from the lemons.

In a bowl, whisk the eggs while adding the sugar, 1 tablespoon at a time. Continue to beat until the mixture is lemony in color. Gradually add the lemon juice and zest.

Transfer the egg mixture to the top of a double boiler, over boiling water brought to a simmer. Slowly whisk in the melted butter. Continue to whisk gently while the mixture cooks. It will appear light yellow and slightly foamy on top, then as the mixture heats and thickens, it will become dark yellow. Cook until it thickens and coats the back of a spoon.

Remove from the heat and, while still hot, pour through a fine-mesh strainer into a clean container. It will keep up to 1 month if covered and refrigerated, but for best quality, use within 2 weeks.

MAKES 2½ TO 3 CUPS.

Bachelor's Jam

In an earlier age, when debutantes gathered in the drawing room for a cup of Darjeeling tea, they would drizzle a bittersweet orange sauce over their tea cakes and biscuits. The bachelors would settle in the library and accent their conversations with sips of brandy and liqueurs. This jam brings the bachelors and the ladies together.

2 tablespoons granulated sugar
1 tablespoon long orange zest strips
1 cup boiling water
1 cup orange juice
1/2 cup orange marmalade
1 tablespoon Grand Marnier liqueur

IN A SMALL, DRY, HEAVY SAUCEPAN, COOK THE SUGAR OVER medium heat. Do not stir. When the sugar begins to melt, slowly stir it until it turns golden. Remove from the heat.

Place the orange zest in a 1-cup measure with the boiling water. Let the zest sit for 20 seconds, then drain.

Return the melted sugar to medium heat. Whisk in the orange juice and zest until blended. Whisk in the marmalade. Remove from the heat and stir in the Grand Marnier. The jam will have the consistency of a syrup.

MAKES ABOUT 1 1/2 CUPS.

Sunny Morning Relish

This sweet relish is especially good on Kathlyn's Gingerbread Waffles (page 27) or as an accompaniment with Cardamom Spice French Toast (page 26).

3 to 4 large navel oranges
2 tablespoons Grand Marnier
    liqueur
2 cups fresh strawberries,
    hulled and sliced
2 tablespoons granulated sugar
1/2 cup currant jelly
1/4 teaspoon freshly squeezed
    lemon juice, or to taste

PEEL THE ORANGES AND CUT CROSSWISE INTO 5 OR 6 SLICES. Layer the slices in a shallow serving bowl and drizzle with the Grand Marnier. Cover and refrigerate.

In a small bowl, combine the strawberries and sugar. Allow the mixture to sit at room temperature for 30 minutes.

Melt the jelly in a small saucepan over medium-low heat. Add the lemon juice. Pour the warm jelly over the strawberries and mix well. Spoon the strawberries and sauce over the oranges. Refrigerate for 1 to 2 hours before serving. To store, place in a covered container in the refrigerator. For best quality, use within 3 days.

MAKES 1 1/8 CUPS.

Cardamom Custard Sauce

*T*his spicy-sweet custard sauce has the heavenly aroma and flavor of whole cardamom seeds, a spice native to India and a member of the ginger family.

4 large egg yolks
3 tablespoons granulated sugar
2 cups half-and-half
3 whole cardamom pods, crushed
1/4 teaspoon vanilla extract

IN A BOWL, WHISK THE EGG YOLKS AND SUGAR UNTIL THICK and light yellow.

In a small, heavy saucepan, heat the half-and-half and cardamom over medium heat until small bubbles appear around the edges of the pan. Slowly whisk the hot liquid into the yolk mixture, then pour into the top of a double boiler. Cook over water that has been brought to a boil and reduced to medium, stirring constantly with a wooden spoon, until the custard thickens and covers the back of the spoon, about 10 minutes.

Strain the custard through a fine-mesh sieve into a clean container. Stir in the vanilla. Serve warm or chilled. It will keep 3 days if covered and refrigerated.

MAKES ABOUT 2 CUPS.

Spiced Blueberry Sauce

I like this sauce over pancakes and waffles, but it's also delicious as an ice-cream topping or as an accent to savory entrées such as lamb or pork tenderloin.

4 cups fresh blueberries
2 teaspoons ground ginger
1 teaspoon ground cinnamon
1/4 cup granulated sugar
1 tablespoon water
1 tablespoon freshly squeezed
    lemon juice

IN A HEAVY SAUCEPAN, COMBINE THE BLUEBERRIES, GINGER, cinnamon, sugar, water, and lemon juice. Bring the mixture to a boil over medium heat, stirring occasionally. Let it boil slowly, until thickened, about 5 minutes. Remove from heat and serve warm.

MAKES ABOUT 2 CUPS.

Val's Molasses Ice Cream

Tigertail Val used to serve the neighborhood kids rich molasses ice cream on top of his warm gingerbread (page 15). I've never forgotten its taste, and I hope I've re-created its enchantment here.

2 cups (1 pint) vanilla ice cream, softened
1 tablespoon light molasses
1 tablespoon cognac

IN A BOWL, COMBINE THE SOFTENED ICE CREAM, MOLASSES, and cognac until well blended. The volume of ice cream will decrease slightly when it softens. Transfer to a container with a cover, return to the freezer, and freeze for at least 6 hours or until ready to use. For best quality, use within 1 week.

MAKES ABOUT 2 CUPS.

Cinnamon Ice Cream

When you combine a rich vanilla ice cream with cinnamon, you create an incredible flavor that makes a cool, delicious accompaniment to gingerbread. For those who like hot fudge sundaes, try this cinnamon ice cream and top it with a handful of toasted almonds.

2 cups (1 pint) vanilla ice cream, softened
2 teaspoons ground cinnamon

IN A BOWL, COMBINE THE SOFTENED ICE CREAM AND CINNAMON until well blended. The volume of ice cream will decrease slightly when it softens. Transfer to a container with a cover, return to the freezer, and freeze for at least 6 hours or until ready to use. For best quality, use within 1 week.

Variation: To make Ginger-Cinnamon Ice Cream, stir in 2 tablespoons coarsely chopped ginger preserves.

MAKES ABOUT 2 CUPS.

Ginger-Lemon Ice Cream

Tart lemon curd and sweet, peppery ginger preserves make an unusual and delectable combination. This ice cream tastes divine by itself and is also a sensational filling for the Gingerbread Cookie–Ice Cream Sandwiches (page 65).

2 cups vanilla ice cream, softened
2 tablespoons purchased lemon curd or
   homemade Lemon Curd (page 74)
1 to 2 tablespoons ginger preserves
   (see Note)
½ teaspoon ground ginger

IN A BOWL, COMBINE THE SOFTENED ICE CREAM, LEMON CURD, ginger preserves, and ground ginger until well blended. The volume of ice cream will decrease slightly when it softens. Transfer to a container with a cover, return to the freezer, and freeze for at least 6 hours or until ready to use. For best quality, use within 1 week.

Note: Ginger preserves can be found in most supermarkets in the jam and marmalade section or in the gourmet section. One popular brand is James Keiller & Son, Dundee Ginger Preserve.

MAKES ABOUT 2 CUPS.

Gingerbread Houses

Our First Gingerbread House

ere is a simple gingerbread house that you can make with your favorite child. Once the pieces are baked, it will easily go together in an hour or two, depending on how you both decide to decorate it.

1 recipe Basic Gingerbread House Dough
  (page 89)
1 set Simple House Pattern (page 92)
Crushed hard candy for colored window
  panes (optional)
Tray or board, at least 8 by 11 inches,
  for displaying the house
1 recipe Meringue Royal Icing (page 90)
Decorations, as needed (see page 85)

PREHEAT AN OVEN TO 325 DEGREES F. POSITION A RACK IN THE center of the oven. Grease 2 baking sheets, and set aside.

To cut out the gingerbread pieces, place a sheet of parchment paper on a work surface. Using a lightly floured rolling pin, roll out one-third of the dough ⅛ inch thick on the paper. Place pattern A (front piece) on top of the dough and, using a sharp paring knife, cut around the edges of the pattern. Carefully lift the pattern off the dough, and cut a second pattern A (back piece).

Remove any excess dough. (The excess dough can be saved and rerolled.) Transfer the paper with the cutout pieces onto a greased baking sheet. Once in place, gently arrange the pieces so there is 1 inch around each piece to allow for expansion during the baking. Create windows and doors by cutting them out of the unbaked dough. For colored panes, drop crushed hard candy into the window space during the last 10 minutes of baking.

Bake until the pieces are set or the edges are slightly brown, about 15 minutes (the time will depend on the size of the gingerbread piece). Remove from the oven and place the baking sheet on a counter. Let the pieces cool for 8 to 10 minutes before transferring to a wire rack to cool completely.

Repeat the same procedure for the remaining dough and other pattern pieces: 2 side wall pieces (B), 2 roof pieces (C), and the chimney (D and E).

To assemble, have ready a sturdy board or tray on which you will build and display the gingerbread house. Holding the pattern A piece that will serve as the front of the house, pipe a generous amount of icing along the bottom edge (aa). Place this section on the display board where you want the house to stand. Prop the piece with small jars until the icing has hardened, about 5 minutes.

To attach the side wall (B), pipe icing along the bottom edge (ff) and along one side edge (gg). Gently attach the side wall to the front piece by pressing slightly. If necessary, prop with small jars until the icing has hardened, about 5 minutes. Repeat with the second side wall (B).

To attach the back side (A), pipe icing along the bottom edge (aa) and side edges (bb and cc), using the same technique. Gently attach to the side walls by pressing slightly. If necessary, prop with small jars until the icing has hardened, about 5 minutes. Before attaching the roof, pipe some additional icing along the inside bottom edges of the house (aa and ff) where the walls meet the display board.

To attach the roof (C), pipe icing along the upper edges of the front and back pieces (cc and dd) and along the upper edges (hh) of the side walls. Gently press 1 roof piece against the icing so that it meets at the peak and has a $\frac{1}{2}$-inch overhang or eaves. If you need to prop the piece until it dries, use tall jars. Repeat with the remaining roof piece. Pipe additional icing to cover the joints. After the roof has set, you can add the chimney.

To create the chimney, use the technique described above to make a small box out of the D and E pieces, with the E pieces parallel to one another and the D pieces parallel to one another. Attach the chimney to the peak of the roof. Pipe additional icing to cover the joints.

To decorate the roof, pipe icing to resemble shingles or thickly spread icing with a spatula, swirling it with the tip of the spatula, to resemble snow. Before the icing hardens, gently push down cookies or candies in any pattern you wish. Pipe icing onto the walls to make windows and the door. Use dollops of icing to attach other decorations onto the walls (see Delectable Decorating Ideas).

Delectable Decorating Ideas

For the roof:
Almonds, raw or sliced
Gumdrops and jellies
Cookies
Mini shredded wheat or square
    cereal pieces
Miniature marshmallows
Round wafer candies
Nonpareils
Orange-wedge jellies
Red licorice
Round peppermint candies
Shredded coconut
M&Ms
Wheat crackers

For the chimney:
Peppermint sticks
Raisins
Red Hots
M&Ms
Good 'n' Plenties

For a chimney alternative:
Graham crackers cut to pattern size
Large straight pretzels for
    standing chimney

For a steeple or spire:
Inverted ice-cream cone with a
    pointed tip
Nuts and chocolate-coated raisins
    for stones on a chimney

For the shutters:
Cookie dough cut into small
    rectangular pieces
Peppermint sticks, 2 or 3 to a side
Short stick pretzels, 2 or 3 to a side
    (they also make window frames)
Small candy canes
Sugar cookie wafers
Unwrapped sticks of gum, striped or
black licorice

For the pathways:
Coffee grounds
Golden raisins
M&Ms
Small jelly beans
Matchstick pretzels
(also for paths and bridges)

For the fences:
Cinnamon sticks
Giant gumdrops
Large or matchstick pretzels cut to
    size for vertical stakes; longer
    pretzels for horizontal stakes
Marshmallows
Small Tootsie Rolls for vertical stakes

For landscaping:
Coffee grounds for dirt
Foil-wrapped chocolate eggs or
    sugar-coated almonds for boulders
Giant green gumdrop on a medium
    pretzel stick for a tree or bush
Green-tinted flaked coconut
    for grass
Inverted ice-cream cones with a
    pointed tip, frosted green or white,
    for trees
Disk-shaped lollipops and ball-shaped
    lollipops for trees

**For a snow-covered
wood pile:**
Large or matchstick pretzels glued
    together with white icing
Cinnamon sticks glued together with
    white icing

Tips for Assembling a Gingerbread House

∗ If the pieces seem too soft before assembling, or if they have absorbed any moisture, place in an oven preheated to 200 degrees F for 10 minutes to harden. Cool before using.

∗ While you will want to pipe a generous amount of icing to secure the house to the display board, use less to mortar the gingerbread pieces together. Too much icing will cause the pieces to slide against each other.

∗ Once the house is built, you can pipe additional icing to cover uneven joints or cracks.

∗ If you are worried about stability, you can attach 2 ice-cream sticks to the inside of each wall by piping icing along the length of each stick. Gently press each stick against the wall so that it is perpendicular to the base, and allow it to dry. Just make sure that the sticks don't show beyond the upper edge of the walls.

Lickety-Split Log Cabin

One Christmas when I was a child, our next-door neighbors, the Neumans, made a gingerbread log cabin. When my grown son, Matthew, was a child, we tried to re-create it. We pressed logs of rolled dough into the shape of the simple gingerbread house we normally made together. It wasn't as intricate, but it worked. Here are the directions for that rustic log cabin. If you want to surround it with a forest of trees, pipe green-tinted icing around a grove of inverted ice-cream cones. For a finishing touch, set a few reindeer cookies peeking out from between the trees.

1½ recipes Basic Gingerbread
   House Dough
1 set Simple House Pattern
Water, as needed
1 recipe Meringue Royal Icing

PREHEAT AN OVEN TO 325 DEGREES F. POSITION A RACK IN THE center of the oven. Grease 2 baking sheets, and set aside. Divide the prepared dough into 3 portions, keeping the unused portions covered with plastic wrap until ready to use.

To create the front piece, place a piece of parchment paper on a work surface. The paper will make it easier to roll out the dough and move it onto the baking sheet. Shape 1 portion of dough into 17 ropes, each 5 inches long and ½ inch thick. Beginning at the bottom of pattern A, position the logs on top of the template, centering them so that each log is parallel to the one above it. As you lay each log on the template, gently press it against the next log. Using a sharp paring knife, cut down each of the sides (cc and dd) to make a 4-inch edge for the peaked roof. Do not cut the edges of the remaining logs. They should remain rounded for a more authentic look.

Carefully lift the logs and the template, and transfer to a greased baking sheet. Once in place, gently slide the template out from under the logs, and adjust the logs as necessary. Brush the dough lightly with water.

Repeat to create the back of the log cabin (pattern A).

Bake until the logs are set or the edges are slightly brown, about 20 minutes. Remove from the oven and place the baking sheet directly on a counter protected from the heat by a towel.

Let the pieces continue to cool for 10 minutes on a flat surface before transferring to a wire rack to cool completely (a wire rack can give warm pieces a rippled surface).

To create a side wall, on a lightly floured work surface, shape another portion of dough into 10 ropes, each 7 inches long and ½ inch thick. Beginning at the bottom of pattern B, position the logs on top of the template, centering them so that each log is parallel to the one above it. As you lay each log on the template, gently press it against the next log. Using a sharp paring knife, cut each side (gg and ii) to make a clean edge. Carefully lift the logs and the template and transfer to a greased baking sheet. Once in place, gently slide the template out from under the logs, and adjust the logs as necessary. Brush the dough lightly with water.

Repeat to create the other side wall (pattern B).

Bake until the logs are set or the edges are slightly brown, 20 to 25 minutes. Remove from the oven and place the baking sheet directly on a counter protected from the heat by a towel.

To create the roof and chimney, place a sheet of parchment on a work surface. The paper will make it easier to roll out the dough and move it onto the baking sheet. Using the remaining dough, roll it out $\frac{1}{8}$ inch thick. Place pattern C on top of the dough. Using a sharp paring knife, cut around the edges of the pattern. Carefully lift the pattern off the dough, and cut out a second roof piece. Transfer the parchment paper with the cutout pieces onto a greased baking sheet. Repeat the same technique for the chimney pieces (D and E).

Bake until the gingerbread is set, 10 to 15 minutes. Remove from the oven and let the pieces cool on the baking sheet for 10 minutes before transferring to a wire rack to cool completely.

To assemble and decorate, follow the same techniques described in Our First Gingerbread House (page 83).

Variations: To create windows and a front door, cut out the desired openings freehand, with a sharp knife, before you are ready to bake. Carefully lift the excess dough out with a toothpick or skewer. Return the door section to the baking sheet and bake as directed.

To create a log roof, follow the same technique for forming the side pieces, but do not cut the edges. They should remain rounded for a more authentic look.

Basic Gingerbread House Dough

T *his basic recipe will work for any gingerbread house you decide to make. This dough goes together easily and also makes delicious cutout cookies. For more detailed instructions about rolling out the dough, cutting the pattern pieces, baking, and assembling, see individual recipes.*

4 cups all-purpose flour
1 tablespoon baking soda
½ teaspoon salt
2 teaspoons ground ginger
1 teaspoon ground cinnamon
½ cup vegetable shortening
1 cup firmly packed dark brown sugar
1 cup dark molasses
2 tablespoons milk, or as needed

IN A LARGE BOWL, SIFT OR STIR TOGETHER THE FLOUR, BAKING soda, salt, ginger, and cinnamon.

In a saucepan, combine the shortening, brown sugar, and molasses over low heat. Stir occasionally until the shortening is melted and the sugar is dissolved, but still slightly grainy. Remove from the heat and let the mixture cool to lukewarm.

Gradually add the molasses mixture to the dry ingredients, mixing until well blended. Add enough milk to make a firm dough. Gather the dough into a ball and cover with plastic wrap. Let the dough rest for at least 20 minutes. (When tightly sealed, the dough will keep for up to 1 week in the refrigerator. Bring to room temperature before rolling.)

Preheat an oven to 325 degrees F. Position a rack in the center of the oven. Have ready 2 ungreased baking sheets.

Using a lightly floured rolling pin, roll out the dough ⅛ inch thick and cut out desired shapes. Bake until the edges are slightly brown, about 15 minutes.

Meringue Royal Icing

Meringue Royal Icing is the mortar and cement of gingerbread houses. Because this recipe uses meringue powder, it is completely edible. You'll find meringue powder in the baking section of many supermarkets, specialty cooking stores, or craft stores that carry professional baking supplies.

3 cups sifted powdered sugar
2 tablespoons meringue powder
6 to 8 tablespoons warm water
Food coloring or paste (optional)
Water, as needed

IN A CLEAN AND GREASE-FREE BOWL, BEAT THE SUGAR, meringue powder, and water, with an electric mixer on low speed, until well blended. Increase the speed to high and beat until the icing forms stiff peaks, 6 to 8 minutes. Add food coloring or paste during the last few minutes of beating.

The icing should hold a peak but be pliable enough to flow through the tip of a decorating bag. If the icing is too stiff, add water, $1/4$ teaspoon at a time, until it is pliable.

Use immediately or cover with a damp, clean cloth to prevent the icing from drying out or forming a crust. If you are planning to work in stages, cover the surface with a piece of plastic wrap and refrigerate. The icing can be stored for up to 3 days. Before using, beat to the desired consistency.

MAKES 3 CUPS.

Royal Icing

For years, the decorative icing typically used for gingerbread houses has been Royal Icing. With the health concerns surrounding the use of raw egg whites, this recipe should be used only for display gingerbread houses, and not be eaten.

2 large egg whites
$1/2$ teaspoon cream of tartar
2 cups sifted powdered sugar
Food coloring or paste (optional)
Water, as needed

IN A BOWL, BEAT THE EGG WHITES WITH THE CREAM OF tartar, using an electric mixer, until stiff. Gradually beat in 1 cup powdered sugar. Continue to beat on medium speed for 10 minutes. Add the remaining 1 cup powdered sugar and continue to beat for an additional 10 minutes. Add food coloring or paste, if desired, during the last few minutes of beating.

The icing should hold a peak but be pliable enough to flow through the tip of a decorating bag. If the icing is too stiff, add water, $1/4$ teaspoon at a time, until it is pliable.

Use immediately for house construction; it soon loses its cementing power. If you want to keep any unused icing for later decoration (not cementing), cover the surface of the icing with a piece of plastic wrap and refrigerate. The icing can be stored for 2 days. Before using, beat to the desired consistency.

MAKES ABOUT $2^{1}/_{2}$ CUPS.

Decorating Tips

Creating colored or tinted icing:

* Paste colors are more vivid and come in a broader palette of colors than liquid food coloring. They are available in small jars at craft or specialty cooking stores.

* Add small amounts of color at a time. It's easy to add color; it's impossible to remove it.

* Always make a generous amount of each icing color you want. If you run out, it will be difficult to duplicate your exact shade.

Using a decorating bag:

* A decorating bag, also called a pastry bag, is a flexible, cone-shaped bag that usually comes with an assortment of decorating tips or nozzles. For assembling and decorating a gingerbread house, use a small, plain round tip. Fill the bag by folding back the top to form a 2-inch cuff. Twist the bag near the tip to prevent the icing from running out while you fill the bag. Spoon the icing into the bag until the bag is half full. Unfold the cuff, twist the top closed, and gently squeeze the bag from the top to release the icing. Periodically twist the top of the bag to increase pressure on the remaining icing.

* Zipper-style plastic storage bags make instant, disposable decorating bags. To use, fill with icing, seal, and snip $1/8$ inch off one corner. Gently squeeze from the top to release the icing. To save time, you can make several of these bags at once, each with a different color and size of opening.

Simple House Pattern

Here are the patterns you need for Our First Gingerbread House (page 83) and the Lickety-Split Log Cabin (page 87). Each finished gingerbread house will measure approximately 7 by 5 inches at the base and will stand 8 ¼ inches tall without the chimney. Transfer the patterns onto parchment paper or tagboard. To make a more permanent pattern, you can cover the paper with clear, self-adhesive contact paper. That way, you simply wipe off the patterns and use them again.

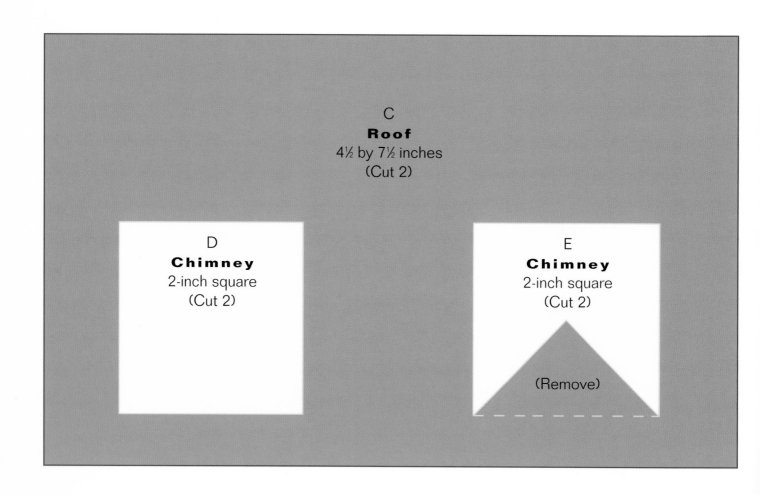

C
Roof
4½ by 7½ inches
(Cut 2)

D
Chimney
2-inch square
(Cut 2)

E
Chimney
2-inch square
(Cut 2)

(Remove)

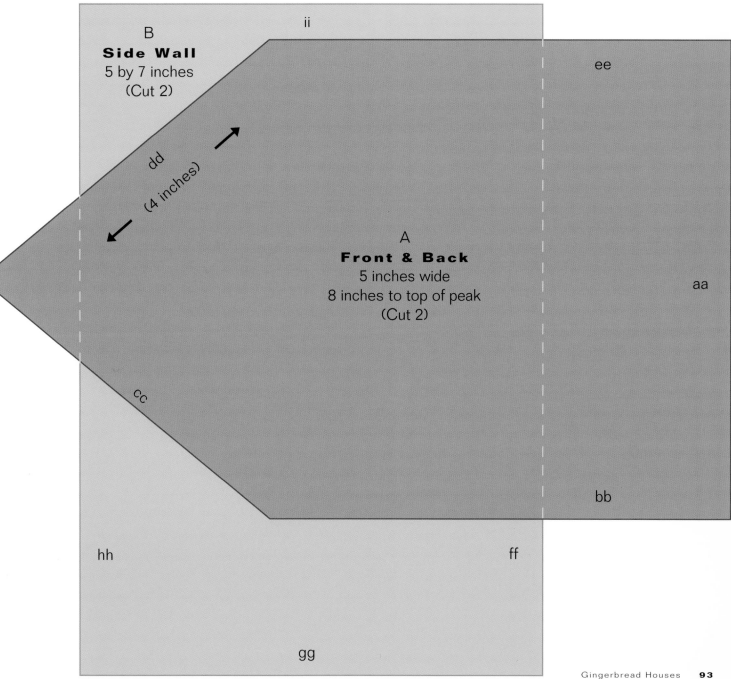

B
Side Wall
5 by 7 inches
(Cut 2)

ii

ee

dd

(4 inches)

A
Front & Back
5 inches wide
8 inches to top of peak
(Cut 2)

aa

cc

bb

hh

ff

gg

Index

Table of Equivalents

The exact equivalents in the following tables have been rounded for convenience.

Abbreviations

US
oz=ounce
lb=pound
in=inch
ft=foot
tbl=tablespoon
fl oz=fluid ounce
qt=quart

Metric
g=gram
kg=kilogram
mm=millimeter
cm=centimeter
ml=milliliter
l=liter

Weights

US/UK	Metric
1 oz	30 g
2 oz	60 g
3 oz	90 g
4 oz (¼ lb)	125 g
5 oz (⅓ lb)	155 g
6 oz	185 g
7 oz	220 g
8 oz (½ lb)	250 g
10 oz	315 g
12 oz (¾ lb)	375 g
14 oz	440 g
16 oz (1 lb)	500 g
1½ lb	750 g
2 lb	1 kg

Oven Temperatures

Fahrenheit	Celsius	Gas
250	120	½
275	140	1
300	150	2
325	160	3
350	180	4
375	190	5
400	200	6
425	220	7
450	230	8
475	240	9
500	260	10

Liquids

US	Metric	UK
2 tbl	30 ml	1 fl oz
¼ cup	60 ml	2 fl oz
⅓ cup	80 ml	3 fl oz
½ cup	125 ml	4 fl oz
⅔ cup	160 ml	5 fl oz
¾ cup	180 ml	6 fl oz
1 cup	250 ml	8 fl oz
1½ cups	375 ml	1 2 fl oz
2 cups	500 ml	1 6 fl oz

Length Measures

⅛ in	3 mm
¼ in	6 mm
½ in	12 mm
1 in	2.5 cm
2 in	5 cm
3 in	7.5 cm
4 in	10 cm
5 in	13 cm
6 in	15 cm
7 in	18 cm
8 in	20 cm
9 in	23 cm
10 in	25 cm
11 in	28 cm
12 in/1 ft	30 cm